# maori sovereignty

## THE PAKEHA PERSPECTIVE

# maori sovereignty

## THE PAKEHA PERSPECTIVE

## CAROL ARCHIE

**Hodder Moa Beckett**

The views expressed in this book are not necessarily those of the
author or publisher.

ISBN 1-86958-209-8

© 1995 Carol Archie

Published in 1995 by Hodder Moa Beckett Publishers Limited
[a member of the Hodder Headline Group]
4 Whetu Place, Mairangi Bay, Auckland, New Zealand

Typeset by TTS Jazz, Auckland
Printed by Griffin Paperbacks, Australia

All rights reserved. No part of this publication may be reproduced or transmitted in any form or by any
means, electronic or mechanical, including photocopying, recording, or any information storage and retrieval
system, without permission in writing from the publisher.

# CONTENTS

| | Page |
|---|---|

**Chapter 1: Hugh Fletcher** – *Chief Executive Officer of Fletcher Challenge.*     11
"There is no chance that Maori are going to get a separate parliament that is going to have any authority over New Zealand. But why worry about that? The authority that a New Zealand parliament has today, as against twenty or thirty years ago, is so small. Increasingly, they've got to run their fiscal and monetary policy to stay within the bounds of what is acceptable to global capital."

**Chapter 2: Bishop John Paterson** – *Anglican Bishop of Auckland and one of the architects of the Tikanga system in the church's new constitution.*     23
"The search for a 'just kawanatanga', for a place to be found for Maori to stand, for the rights and privileges of Maori under the Treaty, is, in my mind anyway, an issue that's really critical to our continued well-being as a society."

**Chapter 3: Glyn Clayton** – *Editor of the* **Christchurch Mail** *and outspoken critic of the Treaty of Waitangi being included in New Zealand law.*     33
"I think it's the fragmentation and the break-up of New Zealand, the end of New Zealand, if we have Maori sovereignty, because we have tribalism and tribalism is what's buggered the world since it began."

**Chapter 4: Mitzi Nairn** – *Director of the Programme on Racism for the Conference of Churches in Aotearoa New Zealand.*     41
"The Declaration of Independence has been one of the best-kept historical secrets. People in our workshops are often excited when they see it, and rightly so, because until you do it is really hard to understand the Treaty of Waitangi."

**Chapter 5: Kevin Smith** – *Conservation Director, Royal Forest and Bird Protection Society.*     53
"There are limits to human rights. The need to protect the environment really can override indigenous people's rights at times."

## Chapter 6: Ken Douglas – *President of the New Zealand Council of Trade Unions.* — 63

*"The process of colonisation was a process of exploitation and theft. That's in its politest sense. There was raping and pillaging and murder and all sorts of things. So those historical wrongs have got to be put right."*

## Chapter 7: Don Riesterer – *Mayor of Opotiki, Vice President of the Local Government Association and Chairman of LGA Maori Consultative Committee.* — 73

*"I think the idea of a separate Maori parliament is a knee-jerk reaction – an easy way out, like a divorce. If your marriage is breaking down it's not easy to sit down and talk the thing through and get it back together again. Perhaps that's one of our troubles in New Zealand. We dissolve partnerships too easily."*

## Chapter 8: Sue Culling – *National Co-ordinator for the funding agency CORSO.* — 83

*"People ask, 'Isn't Maori sovereignty just about giving power to Maori over your life?' I say, 'No. That was never what was envisaged in the Treaty.' Because my ancestors were slaves I'll never be a slave for anybody and I'll never agree to that kind of juxtaposition of power."*

## Chapter 9: Professor Peter Munz – *Professor Emeritus of History at Victoria University.* — 93

*"Assimilation is the essence of human history. You can try to stop it or slow it down but you can't prevent it no matter what you do."*

## Chapter 10: Dr Jane Kelsey – *Associate Professor of Law at Auckland University and informed commentator on Treaty issues.* — 103

*"Sovereignty is the most central critical issue to the future of New Zealand because Maori are mobilising with increasing militancy around it and the more that it is not addressed the stronger those demands and movements will be."*

## Chapter 11: Doug Graham – *Minister in Charge of Treaty Negotiations.* — 113

*"I'm happy to talk about self-management and tino rangatiratanga and what it means, and kawanatanga, all that sort of thing, until the cows come home. But we are not going to waste time on something which isn't going to happen in a country like New Zealand."*

## Chapter 12: Maryan Street – *President of the New Zealand Labour Party.* — 123

*"Maori members of the Labour Party could put up any sensible proposal, argue it cogently, and it would be accepted by the party. There is an absolute willingness to advance legitimate causes of Maori people."*

|   | Page |
|---|---|
| | |

### Chapter 13: Dr Bruce Hucker – *Presbyterian Minister and Alliance Party member of the Auckland City Council.*  133

*"The absence of revolutionary action in New Zealand is a tribute to Maori patience and flexibility which we are going to have to depend on if we are going to have a joint future."*

### Chapter 14: Steven Young – *A Wellington civil engineering consultant of Chinese ancestry.*  143

*"A vague document like the Treaty of Waitangi can say whatever one wishes to make of it. What matters is the weight of numbers and relative strength and who has access to the organs of power. No doubt if Maoris were 90 per cent of the population, the Treaty would be interpreted in a way which was very favourable to the Maoris."*

### Chapter 15: Charmaine Pountney and Tanya Cumberland – *Two professionals, from education and social work backgrounds, who say they are on a journey to support Maori sovereignty.*  151

*"Our support for sovereignty is about learning to be tenants and good neighbours within Ngati Te Ata's rohe. That's our commitment."*

### Chapter 16: George Chambers – *Chairman of the One New Zealand Foundation.*  163

*"There are two hundred pieces of legislation in New Zealand that are discriminatory and the 1974 Treaty of Waitangi Act and the 1984/85 amendments are the worst of the lot. It is the biggest single barrier to harmonious race relations in this country."*

### Chapter 17: Graham Robertson – *President of Federated Farmers.*  173

*"We have to avoid any situation whereby the resolution of these old injustices is going to create new injustices by dispossessing present-day owners, because it is not just Maori who become attached to their land."*

### Chapter 18: Roger Tafa – *A young man of Samoan/European background who supported Maori at Moutoa Gardens and Tamaki College occupations.*  183

*"I support Maori sovereignty. But it is up to Maori to decide for themselves what they mean by sovereignty. Even if that means setting up a separate state, that's something I believe people should support."*

### Glossary  190

# INTRODUCTION

Maori sovereignty is a term which conjures up so many different concepts for so many people. In Maori circles it is often used in an allegorical sense to assert pride, identity and independence; Pakeha frequently find the term unsettling and try to pin it down to something more solid and controllable.

The wide diversity of Pakeha/Tauiwi perspectives on Maori sovereignty will become immediately apparent to readers. It seems there are many areas of New Zealand life where questions of Maori nationhood or self-determination might have an impact and many individual interpretations of how that impact might be felt.

This book is not intended to be an academic discussion analysing the Treaty of Waitangi and its constitutional significance. Nor is it an attempt to describe various new power structures for Maori and Pakeha to consider for the future. Rather it is a collection of very personal views from 19 Pakeha/Tauiwi people who were asked some core questions, around the issue of Maori sovereignty, and then interviewed about their own experience and areas of interest. A person involved in education, for instance, was asked to view Maori sovereignty from an educational perspective; a politician was asked to view it from a political viewpoint; a conservationist from an environmental stance.

All the Pakeha/Tauiwi in the book were encouraged to reflect on their upbringing, education and life experience, and to gauge how it had influenced their thinking about Maori issues. For me, this was the most illuminating and fascinating aspect of the interviews. It was an insight into our recent social history – the general lack of education about our past, the segregated hotel bars and racial discrimination in communities like Pukekohe in the fifties, the sympathy for the "No Maoris No Tour" slogan of the sixties, the challenges presented by Maori activist groups to Pakeha society, the impact of the revisionist histories in the seventies and the way attitudes began to change through the eighties as the injustices of Maori claims to the Waitangi Tribunal became public knowledge.

It sounds obvious when said, but it is worth saying just the same: The extent of people's contact with Maori people and/or their knowledge about Maori issues had a direct bearing on how open they were to discuss Maori grievances and to see them addressed.

It was perplexing to hear a leading businessman say one day that there is no reason why Maori should not have authority (sovereignty) and water rights over an ancestral river and the next day a farmer saying that it would be dictatorship for Maori to own the country's water. Sometimes I felt like a tennis spectator as the various interpretations of tino rangatiratanga and kawanatanga were tossed about. Then, no doubt to puzzle me further, I heard emphatically "We are all New Zealanders" and with equal certainty "How far we all are from being one people"!

The book attempts to provide a balance of views from across the spectrum – young and old, well-known and not so well-known, liberal and conservative. I also selected people who had actually reflected on the meaning of Maori sovereignty and its significance for our society. Everyone will find opinions here to reinforce their own thinking. However, I am sure readers will consider all the opposing or alternative viewpoints as well.

The people featured want to stimulate intelligent debate on Maori sovereignty and its significance for Pakeha in New Zealand. I believe they have given us an insight into current thinking on what kind of nation we wish to build and provided a valuable contribution to start that debate. I thank them all warmly for their frankness, their willingness to be interviewed and the help they gave me in writing this book.

I enjoyed immensely my collaboration with Hineani Melbourne on this venture and wish to thank my husband, Bill, most of all for his honest criticism and unfailing support.

## HUGH FLETCHER

*"THERE IS NO CHANCE THAT MAORI ARE GOING TO GET A SEPARATE PARLIAMENT THAT IS GOING TO HAVE ANY AUTHORITY OVER NEW ZEALAND. BUT WHY WORRY ABOUT THAT? THE AUTHORITY THAT A NEW ZEALAND PARLIAMENT HAS TODAY, AS AGAINST TWENTY OR THIRTY YEARS AGO, IS SO SMALL. INCREASINGLY, THEY'VE GOT TO RUN THEIR FISCAL AND MONETARY POLICY TO STAY WITHIN THE BOUNDS OF WHAT IS ACCEPTABLE TO GLOBAL CAPITAL."*

*Since 1987 Hugh Fletcher has been Chief Executive Officer of Fletcher Challenge Limited, a company with an annual revenue of $10 billion. Prior to that he was Managing Director and Chief Operating Officer for the group's New Zealand activities.*

*Fletcher Challenge is in the pulp and paper, energy and building businesses. The group's involvement with natural resources has brought it in contact with indigenous people not just in New Zealand but in other places where it operates, such as North and South America.*

*In the late sixties, when the company was expanding its forestry operations, it made some of the last purchases of Maori land through the Maori Land Court. It also invested in some significant joint ventures with Maori in forestry projects.*

*Hugh Fletcher first began to think about Maori issues at that time and as more Maori people joined the workforce.*

*He was born in Auckland in 1947 and educated at King's College where Maori history taught him "the colonial attitude towards natives" and how the Maori "were wrong, were obviously impeding progress, and Queen Victoria's British Army sorted it all out". Later he received a MCom and BSc in Mathematics from Auckland University and an MBA from Stanford University, USA.*

*Hugh is married to High Court Judge, Sian Elias, and has two adult sons.*

Hugh Fletcher often attends Maori functions and meets Maori people as the spouse of Sian Elias.

Sian is a prominent New Zealand figure in her own right. She has recently been appointed as a High Court Judge. She was the first woman in this country to become a Queen's Counsel, and one of the youngest. She has been a key player in the legal battles fought by Maori in the Waitangi Tribunal and courts since the mid eighties.

Sian Elias has appeared for claimants to the Manukau Harbour, for the Maori Council in its historic State Owned Enterprises case to the Court of Appeal and the equally historic Maori fisheries claim, the Maori Broadcasting appeal to the Privy Council and the Maori electoral option appeal, also to the Privy Council.

Hugh Fletcher says a lawyer has to keep an element of detachment so he is not sure where, in the spectrum, Sian's views would be. It is his guess that there is very little difference between his views and hers on Maori issues – except hers are more knowledgeable.

As a businessman, the association with Sian's career has given Hugh Fletcher a unique perspective on Maori issues. He says it is generally true that business people know very little about the Maori question "because business is such a time-consuming occupation. Not just in your work hours – the reading you have to do, which is very enterprise-specific – but also the amount of reading you have to do in general, in relation to business. And it doesn't leave you with a lot of time to research, in depth, other topics."

When Hugh talks about sovereignty he says it is something that all New Zealanders are surrendering these days – mostly by choice. He says New Zealanders are choosing to move their sovereignty from a national arena to an international one. At the same time, however, he says they are clawing back more individual freedom from the state "because a lot of that power given to nation states ended up being used to restrict the freedom of individuals".

So, to his mind, Maori are clamouring for something that is becoming less and less important. "The nation state is the thing that is withering in the world today. We're either going local or we're going international. I think Maori should focus on an increased authority at a local level. Why shouldn't the local tribe have authority over the Whanganui River?"

He contends that the one thing Maori did give up in the Treaty of Waitangi was sovereignty – in a national and an international sense. However, he says they did not give up local authority – and Maori sovereignty should be seen as a local issue.

"I personally think they do themselves a lot of damage in running the more extreme sovereignty arguments. I don't think they have the sympathy of the public – nor will they ever get it."

Tino rangatiratanga means chieftainship or tribal authority in Hugh's mind. He says it is like family authority. If a family grouping wants to set processes that govern the way they behave, they are entitled to do so and to have this recognised by the laws of New Zealand.

He says a Maori grouping such as this could replace a local body. "Why not? I don't see why we should feel threatened by our own local council. That's where I think the issue is. It's at that level."

In Fletcher Challenge, staff are encouraged to feel affinity first with their immediate work environment and particular company – whether it be Firths, Placemakers or Tasman Pulp and Paper – and only secondly to feel affinity for Fletcher Challenge as a whole. Similarly, Hugh says a Maori can say: "My first affinity is to my tribe, then to New Zealand." He says there is evidence to suggest that humans prefer smaller groups rather than larger groupings.

However, he believes there is a still role for a national parliament. For instance, no grouping has the right to murder. "But the national parliament must be encouraged to confine that to principles and not detail.

"There is no chance that Maori are going to get a separate parliament that is going to have any authority over New Zealand. But why worry about that? The authority that a New Zealand parliament has today, as against twenty or thirty years ago, is so small. Increasingly, they've got to run their fiscal and monetary policy to stay within the bounds of what is acceptable to global capital."

Only if New Zealanders are prepared to give up a significant chunk of their standard of living can they opt out of the global economy, according to Hugh. "Eventually Westerners have got to understand that the Asians are going to put economics before human rights, because they actually think in terms of mass human rights before individual human rights. So New Zealanders aren't going to give up their standard of living to go back to trying to be a fortress economy in a world that is more global. Given that, national governments are going to become less and less powerful."

While he would confine the concept of Maori sovereignty within strictly local boundaries, Hugh has a much more expansive view of the rights of Maori to claim for their loss of land and resources. In this area he says the Maori expectation is not high enough. The amount spent on the Tainui settlement was less than half the cost of a frigate, which is "pretty mean" in his opinion. So the billion dollars set aside to settle all Maori claims is "mean" also.

"Obviously the fiscal cap was to give Tainui some comfort – that they wouldn't be made to look silly by future settlements – and to facilitate the signing of the first major agreement. And it kind of boomeranged. It became more than the politicians ever really intended it to be.

"We've still got a minimalist Treasury accountant's attitude to the issue rather than a visionary, national attitude."

He has sympathy for tribal representatives who are asked to make a final and binding settlement. "I think it's for them to decide whether they think that is right. After all, one generation signed the Treaty and so another generation is entitled to re-negotiate the Treaty, presumably, or to re-write a clause. I think that means they have to feel that they have a decent deal on whatever they sign away. If they are signing away their rights to resources, then have they got fair compensation for that contractual variation? In that respect, I find the numbers being talked of hard to reconcile with adequate compensation."

If Maori are making deals that future generations will not accept, Hugh Fletcher calls it a "great shame". He says it is undesirable, if you are entering contracts, to have any right to come back and rewrite the bargain. That is why he is so critical of the government's attitude of trying to minimalise the settlements.

"It is better to err on the side of generosity so that you increase the certainty of it being a final settlement, than it is to save a hundred million now and, in fact, not settle the matter. Because before long it will be seen to have been an unfair bargain."

Hugh also disagrees with other aspects of the government's fiscal envelope package, such as the Crown's refusal to consider claims for natural resources and the conservation estate.

"I think that's an outrageously arrogant attitude! It's the viewpoint that:

'Only a New Zealand government set up quango is capable of having conservation principles – Maori aren't to be trusted.' I may not be right on this, but my understanding is that if you actually go into the local communities on, say, the Whanganui River, there is very little concern that if the Maoris were given the river that they wouldn't manage it every bit as well as the Department of Conservation. But, of course, an arrogant Wellington believes they can administer anything better than anyone and are the only ones to be trusted."

He contends that if Maori have a claim then they have a claim. So the government should not preclude the conservation lands.

"In many of these situations I ask: What if Fletcher Challenge had this claim? What attitude would we take? I tell you, if we had a contract that said we had 'full, exclusive and undisturbed possession' of our fisheries we wouldn't settle for the percentage the Maoris have got. It seems pretty unambiguous to me, that wording [from the English version of the Treaty of Waitangi]."

Hugh sees it in more than just the property sense. "I think there is the question of: What is our vision of New Zealand as a nation? In that sense, I think it is bicultural and we should rejoice in it being bicultural – and not wish to make it monocultural."

He has heard about Maori opposition to the sale of Crown lands which might have been used to settle claims and he says it may be Pakeha logic that says, "Just give the people the money and if they want to buy land they will buy land."

"It's possible that somebody else may take a viewpoint that land is different than money and land in a particular location is different from money – that there's a symbolic difference. I mean, that same Pakeha logic says you can't own a river. But who said you can't own a river? That's just the way we think. We haven't bought the idea of property rights to a river but there's nothing philosophically, inherently right, about that Pakeha view.

"It is centuries of the market-based economy which says everything can be put in dollar terms. There's an inability in Wellington, I think, to break out of our way of thinking – and that's a shame."

Looking at other claims to natural resources, Hugh believes Maori may not have a strong case to claim petroleum and gas, but he says the Maori geothermal claim is very strong.

If Maori were to succeed in claiming natural resources like gold, oil and gas he cannot see any conflict for companies like Fletcher Challenge.

"I don't think the issue is really with the developer and producer. I think the issue is with who is obtaining the benefit – the owner. If Maori win their case, we pay the royalty to them rather than paying the Crown.

"In the case of land ownership we have accepted that Maori do own significant tracts of land and may well own more, and that's fine. With the forest crop that we bought off the Crown, we are currently paying land rental into a trust which is held for Maori. If instead we paid it straight to the Maori that would be fine."

Fletcher Challenge owns the major part of a forest in the Tarawera area which is under Maori claim. The forest company which owns the land has an 80 per cent Fletcher Challenge shareholding and the rest is owned by the Crown and some Maori tribes. It is a complex situation where several tribes in the area have claims on it. Some of the land was taken during the land wars and given back, some say, to the wrong tribe.

Hugh is not aware of any other claims on Fletcher Challenge's freehold land although there are a number of claims on Crown forest land over which the company has cutting rights. His attitude to claims on private land is straightforward.

"We paid for fair title and we regard it as ours. If the government wished to buy it then anything's available at a price."

He says Fletcher Challenge would not hold the Crown to ransom and ask an excessive price if the land was required to settle a Maori grievance.

"If there was a unique value, because it was a burial ground or something, we wouldn't do anything other than seek the same value for that property as neighbouring property. In the case of all our properties, I would think establishing value was very easy. There's nothing unique about most of our land in a Pakeha economic sense."

Having said that, Hugh has some concerns about the possible impact of big Maori claims. He says the company has some very large fixed capital investments – worth hundreds of millions of dollars – which require a steady supply of wood. "If somebody wanted to buy all our forests in the central North Island we'd have a bit of a problem, because we have to have the certainty of the wood."

In a case like that Fletcher Challenge would want to retain the cutting rights for at least one more tree crop. After that, he says jokingly, the company might go and plant the East Coast instead "if Forest and Bird will let us!"

Recently the Royal Forest and Bird Society stopped a 50,000 hectare joint venture between Tasman Forestry and Ngati Porou on the East Coast.

The society, which is opposed to the clearing of kanuka shrub lands, had an accord with major forestry companies that they would not clear such areas for pine plantations. They asked the government to subsidise other Ngati Porou areas for planting instead, but after months of talking with all the parties Ngati Porou ended up with nothing.

Hugh Fletcher says the whole issue was unfair to Ngati Porou. He calls it the attitude of "It's all right if I built my bach last year, but you can't build yours this year."

Looking back to the 1960s, when Fletcher Holdings first became involved in joint forestry ventures with Maori, Hugh speaks with some pride. "I think it was one of the first business organisations to really take seriously the question of Maori participation in the economic process. I think very early we took the viewpoint that this was something to be fostered and feel good about and want to do well. We took the Maoris seriously. The joint ventures have been lasting relationships. The real pay-offs are starting now that the wood is being harvested."

More recently, Fletcher Challenge has funded a Maori scholarship programme and invested in the Maori Development Corporation. "We wanted to get Maori more fully involved in the economic process – believing that that would be more conducive to a more harmonious society.

"One of the worrying things is the spotlight is so much on Maori. People love to point out where they have failures or where they have problems. Statistically is it any different? I wouldn't think so. There are a lot of Pakeha families, for instance, who have disputes over matrimonial property and over estates when they die."

The need for Maori to become more involved in the economic process is even greater following the impact of economic restructuring over the last decade. Hugh believes it was inevitable that Maori would suffer disproportionately from the shake-up of industry, because so many were in lower-skilled jobs. He was often critical of the way the restructuring was carried out in the mid to late eighties but he says the outcome would have been the same – a significant number of those jobs would have disappeared.

"If philosophically you are lessening the role of Wellington and the role of regulation and national administrative solutions and relying upon an enterprise-based economy then it is hard to justify trying to come up with centrally administered solutions to one particular component. It's quite possible, if you do, that it will be totally counterproductive. I'm not convinced that even if the government had wanted to devote more resource to this that it would have been particularly effective.

"I personally think there was more to be gained from settling the claims – in giving Maori a greater amount of fish and forests and everything, being more generous in settlements and enabling them to build an employment element into those packages."

His explanation, of why Maori are so predominant in unskilled employment, goes back to last century in the 1830s to 1860s when Maori were adjusting to an economic and trading society successfully, particularly in things like growing food. Then, he says, they were decimated in numbers, in economic status and in health. "Through the decades we slowly ensured we got disproportionate positioning within the economy. You cannot defend our history. But the question is what do you do now?"

He says he is no expert on how one fixes decades of explicit and implicit discrimination but he tends to favour the "old 1960s American school". This means affirmative action policies which make enterprises legally obliged to pursue equality. "Which is essentially where we've gone on the question of sex discrimination – put the real legal bite onto employers to protect themselves against charge."

He believes unemployment and its social impact must bring added tensions to New Zealand society. "You've only got to look at the proportion of the population in prisons and the growing concern people have about crime. Inevitably you are going to have racial overtones in it. You've just got to work away at trying to get the unemployment down, particularly the long-term unemployment.

"And that's where I think forestry has potential. We should be trying to unlock money in the Crown forest rental trust fund and applying it to growing the Maori-owned forest estate – employing Maoris in places like the East Coast. And at some point you've got to knock down a bit of kanuka. I think kanuka is a fantastic tree but it is still less important than people."

Hugh predicts that the gap between rich and poor in New Zealand will continue to widen, as it has worldwide. He says the gap has been opening up faster in this country because New Zealand incomes were more equal in the past and are now moving towards the international averages. He says the huge pools of low-cost labour opened up in Asia have pushed up the demand for capital and lowered the value of labour. Meanwhile high-skilled labour is being paid more.

He expects the bulk of Maoridom to be pushed further down the economic ladder – until they can join the more skilled labour force. "I think you will see another couple of decades in which you'll get very minimal movement in the standard of living in the lower quartile of employment. That's what they've had in America for the last fifteen years – in fact some slight deterioration in real incomes in the lower quartile."

The social impact created by unemployment and low incomes in America may also be hard to avoid in New Zealand, he says. "It's a global force. You've got to take the Singaporean approach and drive employment into higher skilled jobs. And the most important element in that is training."

Fletcher Challenge has dramatically increased internal learning programmes because, Hugh says, increasingly enterprises are realising the intense productivity gains they must achieve. They have to work co-operatively with their staff and up-skill their people.

"It starts with ensuring literacy and basic numeracy and statistical understanding, going on into teaching computer skills. All these people are going to have to interface with computers. Encouraging them to participate in work – rather than just go to work."

While Hugh Fletcher favours positive discrimination legislation to assist Maori to catch up in the work force, realistically he does not expect the government to legislate for it, nor does he see much evidence of it happening on a voluntary basis among most employers. In Fletcher Challenge he says they could fairly claim to be at least equal. Graduate recruitments and training programmes are now "in the right proportions" across the sexes and races.

A more recent development in Maori activism has been to protest against the growth of overseas investment and control. Hugh cannot see why Maori should be any more concerned about this issue than other New Zealanders. He asks why an overseas owner is different from any other non-tribal owner of land.

As a New Zealander, however, he is concerned about foreign ownership. But first of all, he says, New Zealanders must accept that the fault is their own. "We want to consume more than we produce. If we stop doing that then we don't need foreign capital. At the moment that capital is all coming in the form of buying assets or shares."

He acknowledges that it is non-Maori who consume the predominant amount in New Zealand and therefore it is largely non-Maori who are creating the need for foreign capital. "We are running a balance of payments deficit of two to three billion dollars at the moment. If you're goin to contract the economy by that amount, whether it is fair or not, a large chun of that pain is going to fall on the less fortunate, rather than the mo fortunate."

When Maori and other groups protested at the 1995 Asian Developme Bank conference in Auckland the government was concerned about the impa on foreign investors. Hugh, on the other hand, thinks protests are good and th the government should not be so precious. He believes such protests will n influence foreign investors at all. He says they are more likely to be wary MMP – in particular the policies of the Alliance Party – and what that mig mean in terms of legislative change to affect the value of their investments.

Even if Maori were to convince the government to sit down and talk abo sovereignty, Hugh Fletcher cannot see it causing instability for New Zealan in the international market-place. He points to Canada where there was a re prospect that a third of the country might secede. "Canada is surviving tha Put against that, even if they did hold talks on sovereignty, would it make th slightest different to how Don Brash [Governor of the Reserve Bank] rur interest rates and what our fiscal surplus is?

"I think there is recognition all around the world that the indigenous peop are going to get bigger settlements of their claims than they have had i previous decades. You see that in Australia with the Mabo decision. So what The New Zealand government wrote off $2 billion on New Zealand Refinin The whole of the Maori settlements are no more than that. You've got to kee it in proportion."

He says this demonstrates the government's "petty financial thinking" an suggests that their motive for keeping a fiscal cap on Maori settlements is mor political than economic. If Hugh held the government's purse strings he woul make much more generous settlements of Maori claims.

"The whole of Tainui hasn't been settled, because they haven't settled th river. So I would increase the settlement to Tainui, including giving them th river and royalty rights over use of water in the river – for hydro, drinkin water or whatever. And probably do something on coal."

He would apply similar generosity to the Taranaki and Ngai Tahu claim The Bay of Plenty, he believes, can be settled largely through handing ove Forestry Corp land. "They've got a huge asset there – a couple of billion. S they should be able to settle that. Plus they've got dams and the geotherma resource."

In Taranaki where most of the confiscated lands are now in privat farmland, Hugh would give the tribes enough money to buy it back. "The grea bulk of those farmers will sell. If you take fifty years you'll buy the whole place back. I've never met a son or daughter who doesn't have a different view about the property than their parents."

While Hugh is usually struck by how little his colleagues in the business world know about Maori issues, he finds that when the justice of the claims is explained, the arguments get a good reception. "But it starts off with an element of antagonism and ignorance. I think the best way to get the antagonism out is to break down the ignorance."

Hugh believes that good race relations are good for business and he promotes this idea in the business community wherever it is appropriate — at meetings with colleagues, at dinners and lunches.

However, on these occasions he does not support anything other than a local version of Maori sovereignty. "It's my personal view that Maori preoccupation with sovereignty is misdirected and misguided. I just don't have any sympathy with that line."

## JOHN PATERSON

*"The search for a 'just kawanatanga', for a place to be found for Maori to stand, for the rights and privileges of Maori under the Treaty, is, in my mind anyway, an issue that's really critical to our continued well-being as a society."*

**J**ohn Paterson is the Anglican Bishop of Auckland and one of the architects of the Tikanga system which was introduced into the Anglican Church constitution in 1992.

He is a fourth generation New Zealander of Scottish and English extraction, born in Pukekohe in 1945 and raised there during the fifties when it was one of the most openly racist communities in New Zealand. From the third form John travelled by train each day to King's College where he can remember only one Maori pupil during his time there.

In his family Maori were regarded as different. "It was best not to mix with them because you could never really trust a Maori – a vague sort of suspicion from a distance."

However, his father's family, who had lived in Ngaruawahia, spoke of Princess Te Puea with great respect and were proud of a greenstone pendant she had presented to his grandfather.

Bishop John Paterson's whole outlook on things Maori began to change when he went to Auckland University in 1963 in preparation for *ordination in the Anglican Church. He lived in a hostel in Parnell with several fellow students who were Maori and he made an unusual decision for the times – to study Maori as part of the "foreign language" requirement for his degree. "It was not popular. I had to convince the church authorities at the time that it was a good thing to do."*

At John Paterson's primary school in Pukekohe they had what was called "the Maori room" and Maori were segregated into that room. He says that lasted until a Maori school was built and the Maori children were taken out of the primary school altogether.

"It was an extraordinary place in the 1950s. Very little chance for mixing of the two peoples or any chance for understanding and trust to develop."

Pukekohe often hit the headlines during that period as a flash point for racial disharmony in New Zealand. The local picture theatre allowed Maori to sit downstairs but not upstairs. Some of the dairies and businesses in the town would not serve Maori. There was a "Maori only" bar at the Pukekohe Hotel.

Looking back, John Paterson believes it was a difficult community because while there were many Maori in the town – and it is clearly in the Waikato tribal area – they were not strongly tribally based. A large proportion of the population came from other areas to work in the market gardens and John says the local marae always seemed to struggle for leadership and support.

As a youngster, John says his attitudes were a good reflection of the misconceptions and misunderstandings of his parents. He started to examine his views and prejudices about Maori when he began studying Stage One Maori at university. He had a choice between Maori language and New Testament Greek, which was very difficult to learn, so he chose Maori – deciding that he was "more likely to mix with and minister to Maori than to ever meet up with a person speaking New Testament Greek."

The Bishop of the day told him it was not a wise decision but later changed his mind and encouraged him to continue with his Maori language studies. When John arrived at St John's Theological College it soon became clear that having studied Maori was useful and something he should pursue further. "We had a lecturer in church history at the time who said to me, 'Can I borrow your Maori studies notes?' His name was Paul Reeves."

Once ordained, John was sent to be the junior curate in the parish of Whangarei where he met an elderly retired priest called Herepo Harawira. The old man was a great orator who had been taught to speak English by studying Shakespeare and the King James version of the Bible.

"He also spoke classical Maori. And he took me under his wing, to tangihanga, to visit old people in the Whangarei district, to holy communion in their homes and that kind of thing. I'd been able to pass an academic paper in Maori but I had absolutely no skills in oral Maori at all. He was the one who really made me feel that perhaps I could minister to Maori because of the way he taught me and nurtured me and, in a sense, protected me from making glaring mistakes."

In 1970, after only 18 months in Whangarei, John was asked to be the pastor in a Maori pastorate in the Nga Puhi area, based in Kaikohe. "The Bishop had quite literally run out of Maori clergy. He asked me to go as an experiment to see if the people would accept a young, inexperienced Pakeha priest."

If he was to succeed in this position John had to pass muster with a key Nga Puhi leader, Eru Pou, who was renowned in the area for his distrust of Pakeha. Eru Pou lived opposite the Maori vicarage where the raw new pastor lived.

John crossed the road to see him soon after he arrived. "He was sitting on his doorstep staring across the road towards the vicarage and he was smoking his pipe and had his tokotoko on the step beside him, sitting in the sun. I went over and approached him and he said to me in English as I was walking up the path: 'Come and sit down here Pakeha, I know who you are.'"

The conversation continued in English and John felt sure he was not doing very well. He told Eru he was in favour of church union and the old man told him he would soon change his mind on that. After an hour, John rose to go, thinking he would have to report to the Bishop that things were not too hopeful.

"I decided to try a little bit of Maori and I think I said something like 'Hei konei ra e te matua.' He picked up his tokotoko and banged it on the step and said, 'E noho, e noho, Pakeha. Now we'll really start to talk.'"

He soon learned that Herepo Harawira and Eru's son, Jim, who worked in the Whangarei Maori Affairs office, had prepared the old man for his visit. It became clear that he would be accepted after all. In fact, over the next nine years, Eru and two other community leaders, Pat and Bea Whiu, taught him a great deal about the house of Nga Puhi, about the people, the marae and their customs, and helped him improve his oral skills with the language.

Another much-loved role model for John during those years was Bishop Manu Bennett who would come up north and stay at the vicarage. "We developed almost a father and son relationship. He's wonderful. Just one of those special people."

From Kaikohe John moved back to Auckland to work with Kingi Ihaka in the Auckland Maori Mission and was appointed as the first full-time chaplain at Queen Victoria School in Parnell.

During his years at Queen Victoria the structural side of the Maori Church came into prominence. The Bishopric of Aotearoa was granted some autonomy in 1978 by the General Synod and it needed a structure to back it up. John Paterson was elected as a member of a body called the Aotearoa Council and asked to be a part-time secretary for the Bishopric. "So right from the beginning I was part of the structure and part of the administrative side of the re-emergence of the Maori Church."

John worked part-time for Bishop Manu Bennett and then with Bishop Hui Vercoe until 1982 when the workload grew too great and he moved to Rotorua to take up the job full time.

He was in a good position to observe some critical steps which began to unfold within the church. In 1984, during the protests at Waitangi, a number of Anglican priests were arrested on the Treaty grounds while protesting about the government's failure to honour the Treaty. It upset Maori church leaders in the north whose ancestors had signed the document. They asked why members of the church were trampling on the mana of their Treaty.

That year the Aotearoa Council took a long motion to the church's General Synod, asking the church to start looking at the Treaty and its implications for the church's own life and structures. As a result a bicultural commission, of three Maori and three Pakeha, was formed with John Paterson acting as its bilingual secretary.

John travelled all over New Zealand with the commission while it listened to submissions from Pakeha, usually in church halls, and from Maori, usually on marae. He says it was fascinating to see how the Pakeha members of the commission were gradually won over by what was happening.

"I'd done some study of the land wars and what happened in the north, because that's where I'd been. I had very little understanding of the raupatu in Waikato and Taranaki. Some of the things that the commission was told about the land wars in Taranaki were a real eye-opener for me. Right through New Zealand there were some very valuable things said to us.

"Part of our task was to be as open and honest as we could about the church's own position and its own land – gained by one means or another from Maori." After the commission's report the Anglican Church returned some of its land to Maori and has tried to redress other injustices it caused.

At that time it was common for liberal church people to talk about how Pakeha should feel guilty for what had happened in the past. John, however, says that guilt is a negative emotion which does no good. "You have to move through that guilt, actually address the wrong-doing, try to meet that injustice head-on and see what can be done about it."

The commission reported to the synod in 1986 and John says that was the watershed for the Anglican Church and its structures.

"Maori sovereignty" was a term little used during this time and still is not widely discussed in the church. Nevertheless the church was aware that if they could achieve some structural revisions and constitutional rearrangements, it could eventually be offered as one model, among others, for the nation to look at.

The structure the church came up with is known loosely as the Tikanga system. It involves three cultural streams called Tikanga. There is the Pakeha church which has seven dioceses, the Maori church (Te Pihopatanga o Aotearoa) which has five main regions and the church in the Pacific, called the Diocese of Polynesia. The Diocese of Polynesia has an important presence in New Zealand but is largely based in Fiji, Tonga, Samoa and the Cook Islands. The three Tikanga meet together in what is called the General Synod (Te Hinota Whanui).

"What the church had to face was how to design a system that was not simply based on the power of numbers – or the game of democracy – as it was in the past. The Maori church had had only a small representation in the General Synod and had always been outvoted on matters of importance because of democracy – one person, one vote, the majority always wins. The Maori church experience was that it was very, very costly for a minority group."

The Tikanga system aims to allow the Maori view to come through and to recognise "tino rangatiratanga". "Similarly, but at a slightly different level, the Tikanga Pasifika cannot be simply outvoted because of their small numbers. The diocese has been part of our church for quite a long time. Although it's not part of the Treaty settlement, we wanted to design a system that acknowledged the Treaty of Waitangi, and the relationship between Pakeha and Maori, and yet also had that third partner in it."

The original church constitution was designed largely by Bishop Selwyn in 1857. It required any act of the diocesan or general synods to be approved by three houses of the church – the bishops, the clergy and lay people. "It in fact ensured for Selwyn, and his successors, almost a power of veto, because if the Bishop doesn't agree, then things don't happen.

"We have added a further layer to that voting pattern. We still have to have the assent of those three houses, but before any particular matter moves to that ordinary vote within the General Synod, any one of the three Tikanga has the right to ask for what we call 'an assent by Tikanga'."

It means that if the Maori church, the Pakeha church or the Polynesian church feel that any particular measure going before the synod impinges adversely on their life, they can ask for a special vote. If any of the Tikanga say "no" to the motion then it does not proceed to the main vote. "And that's the way the rights of any of those partners are protected."

Only two general synods have been held since the new constitutional arrangements were introduced and so far none of the Tikanga groups have chosen to ask for an assent by Tikanga.

John says the procedure hasn't been used because simply having it there makes everyone work much harder at understanding the other point of view. If it looks like there is a difficulty, then the synod has felt that it is far more important to halt proceedings and allow the various groups to reach some kind of consensus.

"The Tikanga voting procedure is not so much a power of veto as a chance for one of the three partners to say to the other two: 'We can see that this is important for you. It is not so for us. By withdrawing at this point we can allow this to happen and for your life to be improved. Do it for yourselves if this is important but don't legislate in that way for us.'"

He admits it sounds complicated but he says the process itself is relatively simple and has been a very good process for the church. It has had the effect of making people work very hard at knowing what their own values and principles are, seeing how that might affect their cultural partners and ensuring a mutual understanding and trust develops.

One fault he sees with the constitutional changes is that new people must be made aware of the reasons behind it so that they do not revert to behaving as they did in the past. "We also have to do some work on how it affects other levels of church life. We tell people in parishes that they should carry on as they are but they should also try to understand why the church at this national level has made these changes."

Critics of the new structure, mainly people in the pews, find it hard to understand why it was necessary to split the church into three.

"They don't appreciate the fact that what we've done by emphasising the unique character of each of those three partners has in fact really freed each of them to be themselves, to develop the life, mission and ministry of the church in ways that are natural and appropriate to them. At certain points when we come together again we are still one – but that unity or oneness is not something we take for granted. It's something you have to work really hard at."

The developments in the Maori church over the past decade have increased Maori numbers in the Anglican Church significantly – at a time when most of the mainstream churches have experienced a decline in congregations. John believes it is because by granting independence to the Maori church its members realise that it is entirely their responsibility to make sure it continues to thrive.

When John joined the Maori ministry in the 1970s, he says there were only about 10 full-time Maori clergy left throughout New Zealand. Nowadays there are more than 300 ordained Maori ministers and at least 250 lay readers.

"Their aim is to try to have a Maori ministerial presence in virtually every marae in Aotearoa – a huge undertaking, which they have very nearly achieved. So there has been a new life. It's a huge development and they're doing some remarkable things."

John is not sure how the Anglican constitution could translate into national political structures. "Our form of sovereignty works for us because we have a common ground. We call it the turangawaewae – the common meeting ground where at some point Maori and Pakeha within the church have a common Christian faith. On the national political level that common meeting ground has yet to be found. There is a lack of trust, a lack of mutual understanding.

"And I think there are many Maori who have almost moved beyond the church pattern of a sense of partnership based on the Treaty. They are now saying, 'We don't even want partnership. We simply want a form of sovereignty which is mana motuhake, minimal contact, our own sense of real control over our own lives in our own way.'"

To his mind, that view of sovereignty will never work. He believes there needs to be some way through the Treaty which accepts the rights of the settler to be in New Zealand – "some way in which a just sovereignty or kawanatanga can be developed together".

"It may be by means of a separate House in which Treaty issues are considered – in which Maori have predominance. It may be in some other way. It may be by simply incorporating the right of each Tikanga – as the church has done – to say 'yes' or 'no' to any particular issue. But I'm personally attracted to the idea of a kind of Upper House in which issues seen to have significance in the Treaty are dealt with in a binding manner by a body in which the Maori voice cannot be outvoted."

John's interpretation of tino rangatiratanga is based on his understanding of the 1835 Declaration of Independence. "I remember Sir James Henare talking to us once about this. He said the tupuna who actually signed the Treaty were very intelligent people and they did so on the basis of the declaration they'd made five years earlier. They were allowing things to happen on the basis of their pride and security in who and what they were as a total people – who were united at that point in understanding that they had the mana, the authority – and that some parts of that chiefly authority could never be divested from them."

He has heard about the opinion of constitutional lawyer Professor Jock Brookfield, who says that because the Crown has assumed power or sovereignty for so long, it has gained legitimacy, no matter how that sovereignty was asserted. For John Paterson that argument has lost ground recently with the Tainui settlement.

"The fact that the government has now, in a major settlement with a major iwi, actually conceded the mistakes and wrongs of the past, and the fact that the government has asked the Crown to issue an apology, suggests that its assumption of credence, its assumption of legitimacy, is not entirely unchallenged. There are chinks appearing in that. I don't think that a government which felt it was entirely legitimate would have gone to such lengths to procure that settlement with Tainui if it really felt that it was absolutely unchallengeable at that level."

John is critical of the government's refusal to discuss sovereignty issues with Maori. He calls it a negative and unhelpful position. He believes there should be some forum provided for such discussions. "It may be, at that point, that the lessons organisations like the church have learned may be brought into play, that the churches might well be consulted."

He believes a difficulty for the government – and maybe for Maori, too – is the lack of any established Maori body to speak for the Maori world, for the various tribal entities and for the people in the cities who don't have automatic entry into iwi structures. "Because without that the government can continue its divide and rule games and simply say, 'Well if they can't agree then we'll just have our own way.'

"The search for a 'just kawanatanga', for a place to be found for Maori to stand, for the rights and privileges of Maori under the Treaty, is, in my mind anyway, an issue that's really critical to our continued well-being as a society. It has to be faced and a way forward has to be found."

He says he does not wish to sound full of gloom and doom but he believes New Zealand is moving into an era when the polite restraint shown by a former generation of Maori no longer holds. He says there is an impatience to achieve settlements, to make progress, being exhibited by this generation. "And I think the rising generation of young Maori – particularly those coming through kohanga reo, kura kaupapa Maori – are going to be strong and proud in a way and in such numbers as we haven't seen for a long time.

"The issues, unless they are dealt with fairly, clearly and in great detail, will become more and more clouded and facts and truth won't be able to stand in the way of people's desire to achieve some kind of settlement, some kind of rearrangement. It may even become quite violent and most uncomfortable for us."

The Pakeha mass media is not meeting its responsibility in this area, in his view. He says they will need to do much better than they have in the past about helping people to understand the issues and see clearly what is going on, "rather than simply reinforcing the negative and giving emphasis to the more provocative stuff without any kind of careful, detailed background."

Often Bishop John Paterson and other church leaders have had difficulty getting the mainstream media to publish material which shows Pakeha supporting Maori issues. This is a grave problem in his view. He says it took too long for any balanced information to be presented through the mass media about the Moutoa Gardens occupation. "How much good material was presented through the *New Zealand Herald*? Not until fairly late in the day was there any kind of balanced stuff starting to come through."

John contends that Pakeha cannot sit back and do nothing about the debate over Maori sovereignty. He says Pakeha need to develop an awareness that they are a partner under the Treaty and that a partner has direct responsibilities.

"I think, for most Pakeha people, that awareness is simply not there.

The commonly held misconception 'We are all one people, what's the fuss?' has got to be addressed. I think it is actually a very dangerous view.

"Pakeha have to be made aware that the oneness they assume can never be assumed – unless it is actually worked at and achieved at certain critical points. In fact we are so far from being one people!"

**GLYN CLAYTON**

*"I THINK IT'S THE FRAGMENTATION AND THE BREAK-UP OF NEW ZEALAND, THE END OF NEW ZEALAND, IF WE HAVE MAORI SOVEREIGNTY, BECAUSE WE HAVE TRIBALISM AND TRIBALISM IS WHAT'S BUGGERED THE WORLD SINCE IT BEGAN."*

**G**lyn Clayton has been Editor of the **Christchurch Mail** for nearly 10 years. The newspaper, owned by the **Christchurch Press**, is published on Tuesdays and Thursdays and has a circulation of 124,000.

His editorials are known for their bluntness and he likes to create controversy. For many years he has been warning his readers about the consequences of including the Treaty of Waitangi in New Zealand law. He believes that assimilation for people of all ancestry is the best course for this country and warns against "separatism" and "apartheid".

Glyn was born in Ashburton in 1933. His maternal grandparents came from Northern Ireland in 1862. His paternal grandfather trained as a doctor in Britain and then came to Rangiora in 1882 where "he did a lot for North Canterbury Maori". Glyn values a carved walking stick given to his grandmother by the local tribe in recognition of his grandfather's unpaid services to Maori.

Glyn has four children from his first marriage and three grandchildren. Recently he married again so he has begun his sixties with a young baby and a toddler.

Glyn Clayton and his mates drink with a Maori train driver in a Christchurch pub every Friday night. "We keep saying to him that he's taking over the bloody country and he won't need us much longer and things like that. He just laughs and says 'Too right man, eh?'" However, Glyn says they are just like any other group of Kiwi guys in the pub – they don't go too deeply into issues like religion and politics.

Glyn has had very little contact with Maori culture in his 62 years. "In my early days, being a South Islander of course, Maori didn't exist. We were just New Zealanders."

At Christchurch Boys' High where Glyn was educated he learnt the "normal" history of New Zealand. "About the Europeans coming and the Maori coming out of Hawaiki – and the canoes. Later the Manning book, *Old New Zealand*. I learnt *Pokare kare ana* and *Now is the Hour* in Maori and hakas for the First XV. It was just a thing you did.

"We were one people and therefore the Maori part of it was just a natural part of one's life. Maori were like the guy next door – no difference. Now we are becoming racist and tribalist and separated.

"I'm of the era where we grew up and thought we were New Zealanders. Now we are Pakeha and Maori. That's not good. Difference creates division."

This philosophy was endorsed for Glyn when he met Louis Armstrong in the early sixties. Being a jazz fan, Glyn was keen to interview one of the jazz greats – and he was especially amused by Louis Armstrong's reply to a question from one reporter.

"Some prissy prick from the *Press* said, 'On the cover of your LP they said that America's secret weapon was a horn player in high C or some such. Do you think your music has done something to bring the east and west together?' And Louis said, 'Ah Jesus!'"

Glyn and a news editor spent the afternoon with Louis Armstrong drinking brandy. "Yeah, he was a good guy. It was a bloody good afternoon. He said: 'God damn, some people say I'm an Uncle Tom but all I do boys is blow a horn.'"

Another anecdote is told to explain what he sees as an obstacle for Maori in pulling themselves out of their unemployment problems. Glyn was working in public relations and writing a house magazine for a big retailer in Auckland.

"They had a very nice young Maori bloke who was their assistant accountant. He was getting his degree and was working well. The boss told me about the latest office romance with this Maori bloke and a

Pakeha girl. But the boss said, 'It won't happen. All his brothers are in a gang in Hamilton and every time he goes home it takes about a fortnight to jolly him back on. They are saying to him all the time, 'Why are you trying to be a Pakeha, boy? Why are you turning against us, eh?'

"He wasn't turning against them. He was just getting on with his life and he could handle the Pakeha way. In the end he just went – gone! Just another one."

Glyn says Maori need peer encouragement to beat unemployment. "They are not unintelligent, God help me. There is a gang idea that anything Pakeha is bad, so if you start to get on you become an Uncle Tom. And therefore you are letting down the Maori way. It's anti-education and anti-white."

Maori unemployment stems from the days when Maori made a major shift from rural areas to cities according to Glyn. He says the only skill they had was muscle and the world doesn't want muscle any longer. "Uneducated muscle is out. No one told the Maori, or they didn't understand that they had to use school to advantage. And a lot of white people were no different in my time."

When the Labour government included the Treaty of Waitangi in legislation in the mid eighties Glyn felt prompted to speak out against it. He began writing tough editorials in the *Christchurch Mail* warning Pakeha about what he saw as the consequences.

"I thought it was all going backwards. We were going back to 1840. Lange got up and said we were going the way of Northern Ireland if we didn't accept there was a special need for Maori and the Treaty had to come into the law. You know I'm half a Northern Irishman. He wouldn't know what he was bloody talking about. I can still hear my grandmother – she didn't like Catholics."

The idea of positive discrimination in education and other areas to help Maori catch up in the system is anathema to him. "So that means if you are a Maori you can take a person's appendix out. You didn't go to that lecture but you are a doctor and it's OK because you're Maori!

"Then came the Race Relations Act and you were told that Maori could criticise everything that Pakehas had done but you couldn't turn around and say that it would be a great country if we got rid of the Maoris because fifteen per cent of them caused eighty-five per cent of the crime."

After Glyn printed what he describes as "an innocuous article" criticising the new Act, the Race Relations Conciliator wrote him a three-page letter. "He indicated that I had been too clever. He wished that the law would provide for him to get shits like me. He didn't call me a shit but that's what he meant."

Talk of Maori sovereignty really gets Glyn Clayton going. He says that is what Maori signed away in 1840. He contends that they signed the Treaty because they needed a higher power. "The chiefs appreciated the advancement of the white and could read what came out of a musket better than most, because they were a warrior tribe. And they were only too keen to have the Treaty of Waitangi because then all the sub-tribes were subjected to the big chief, Queen Vic, even the redcoats and the settlers. Otherwise there was only one answer – no Maori at all. They weren't stupid, you know. Christ, you only had to look at the firepower that came out of the guns on the naval frigates – and they could see more coming."

Glyn claims that the general intent of the document was well understood. He says some tribes did not sign because they had problems with it. They understood it sufficiently to stand aside. Nowadays he calls it typically Maori to question what the Treaty meant.

"If it doesn't suit your argument you say, 'I didn't sign that one.' That's exactly the same argument as the Maori musterer who was skiting about his dogs up in Gisborne. Talking to his Pakeha musterer mate he boasted, 'You know, my dog took seven hundred sheep down to the South Island on his own.' The Pakeha said, 'Oh no he didn't. What about Cook Strait?' And the Maori said, 'He didn't go that way.'"

In a *Mail* editorial last year Glyn Clayton wrote about what he called Pakeha disingenuousness in accepting the present growth of Maori culture and financial wealth.

> Are the Whites of this country really prepared to see a rival culture, language, political and legal system grow up which will be based on the handover of huge tracts of land, sea and money to a few Maori leaders who will enjoy the benefits disproportionately to the returns received by Joe Maori? And of course no return to Pakeha. And does the Maori realise that in this handover lie the seeds of massive discontent, for the wealth is based on race not individualism? The Maori system of chiefs is simply hierarchical which Pakeha abandoned long ago. The Maori as well as Pakeha have gained from Pakeha equality in the eyes of the law and in the way we elect our leaders.
>
> In the long term there is really only one hope for the tribes of New Zealand to live together and that is assimilation of one and all, so we do exist as one people no matter what our ancestry.

On assimilation, Glyn asks, "How can you make laws for Maori and Pakeha with the amount of bonking that's likely to continue even if you don't take into account the amount of mixed blood now? Three hundred years out from now – I mean I haven't got Maori in me but my grandchild has, my nephews and nieces have. You can't separate them out."

In another editorial this year he wrote:

> I have been trying to point out for the best part of ten years that Maori would never be satisfied with a simple adoption of the Treaty of Waitangi. Why in heaven should Maori be satisfied with the Treaty when they have got the chance of taking the whole country? But if we are now a tribal nation, which in my view is exactly what we are, given the Treaty of Waitangi has been cemented into law, who is going to look after the Pakeha tribe?

Glyn's opposition to tribalism is central to his whole argument against the idea of Maori rights. "I think it's the fragmentation and the break-up of New Zealand, the end of New Zealand, if we have Maori sovereignty, because we have tribalism and tribalism is what's buggered up the world since it began."

To his mind tribalism is an uncivilised way of government. He says it has taken centuries of struggle to get a few countries to adopt democracy and the concept of equality. This country, on the other hand, is making every effort to tear down a common or universal approach in favour of the "splintered, blinkered and egocentric".

"And it is being assisted, not only by a selfish few Maori who can see grandeur ahead in taking over Maori leadership, but also by thoughtless Pakeha who somehow believe tribalism will assist Maori into a new dawn. Tell that to the inhabitants of former Yugoslavia and Arab lands torn apart for centuries by various sects and tribes."

Glyn interprets Maori demands for sovereignty to mean separatism. He claims there is no concept of "sharing" or "partnership" in the demands. He calls it a matter of "them and us".

"The Maori denies he gave away sovereignty so he has destroyed partnership. You can't have it both ways. If you agree there's partnership then you accept the sovereignty was signed away. I don't see how any individual who has three-fifths Maori and two-fifths Pakeha can divide their mental processes. How can you have partnership with yourself?

"New Zealand is finished if they give Maori sovereignty because with sovereignty you must talk about law, government and territory. And that's apartheid."

Glyn tells another story he read "in the *Economist* or somewhere in the last 10 years" about an American Indian who had been living in the mainstream of American life and returned to a tribal territory which has self government. "This able-bodied, intelligent redskin" was brought up before tribal law because he was drunk. "And this intelligent adult was given six strokes with the cane. That was tribal law!"

The Maori fisheries claim gets a hammering because he sees it as a transference of wealth into a very very few Maori hands. "And how much of that will percolate down to Joe Maori? I come from a strain of people who've rebelled against the British Crown and the aristocracy and the nineteenth century mercantile class. I'm all for equality and here we are flat out building the reverse. Inequality is the name of the game because you are putting immense financial power into the hands of very few and they happen to be Maori who are accountable by whom to whom? No one!"

He claims Pakeha are handing over the assets of the nation. He wants to know how much will go back into the communal pot for Maori to look after themselves. "If they want a Maori college to teach Maori language in Gisborne why get your hand in my bloody pocket here in Christchurch when we've handed over the asset?

"It may be all right if they build big edifices like Maori language colleges and have people learning about Maori law and Maoritanga but what the hell is that going to do? Make the country more divided? Build false hope? I think it is bloody silly to teach Maori language and culture in this pint-sized nation of 3.4 million. We ought to be learning Cantonese. We've got to survive in this world – not indulge ourselves."

Glyn concedes that there are cases where Maori claims to land are justified. For instance, he says if a bit of land was taken by the government for war purposes, not paid for and then turned into a golf course, the Maori should be paid. However, he would have a cut-off point for claims at about 1900.

"It's all one way at present, isn't it? The white is wrong and the brown is right. Why am I wrong? I was born in 1933. I never had any antagonism to Maori. I'm only too keen for them to get their golf club back if we pinched it from them in some bureaucratic nonsense during the war. Give it to them. But how is it that suddenly I am morally a bloody infidel, eh?

"Maori activists are pathetic. They are just working from a narrow interpretation of moral supremacy or right. The white has got to be honest with himself. We conquered the bloody place. We gave them the Treaty. They weren't shot into the ground. We didn't go out as they did in Tasmania and have an Aborigine shoot after midday on Sunday.

"The reason that I didn't grow up with more Maoris around me is because Te Rauparaha came down here in 1833. It wasn't the Pakeha who knocked them off. It was my bloody grandfather who was trying to keep them alive."

When Glyn talks to other people about Maori claims he says they are sick of being wrong. "These are straightforward decent people. They fought Hitler. A lot of them put their necks on the line. We go on about the Maori Battalion. Christ, they were only a battalion! Do you know how many's in a battalion? Eight hundred to a thousand. And we go on about the Maori in the First and Second World Wars all the bloody time. Christ Almighty, there were half a dozen of them compared with whites. We had three battalions from Canterbury of whites. So did Otago. So did Nelson. So did Southland. You know you've got to put it in perspective."

So he is trying to nudge both sides to think about what is happening. "I'm saying to the Maori: Do you know what you are doing Joe? I'm just holding up a mirror to society.

"People come up to me and say, 'Thank God you are writing this because I always thought that way and never thought anyone else did.' I sound skiting now but I reckon that eighty per cent of those who read my editorials agree with me. You know, the silent majority. It mightn't be eighty per cent but it's a huge majority and I reckon that includes many with Maori blood as well."

MITZI NAIRN

*"The Declaration of Independence has been one of the best-kept historical secrets. People in our workshops are often excited when they see it, and rightly so, because until you do it is really hard to understand the Treaty of Waitangi."*

*S*ince the early seventies, Mitzi Nairn has worked to overcome racial discrimination and inform Pakeha about Maori issues. She was a foundation member of New Perspectives on Race, a community education organisation. In 1988 she became Director of the Programme on Racism for the Conference of Churches in Aotearoa New Zealand.

Mitzi and her psychologist husband, Ray, have been married for more than 30 years and they share the same social agendas. They don't have children so Mitzi has had freedom "to act out our agendas while Ray did the earning."

Born in London in 1942, Mitzi came with her family to settle in New Zealand after the Second World War and lived on a farm. Apart from a few years at Miranda Primary School, which had a large number of Maori pupils, most of Mitzi's education (as a boarder at St Cuthbert's in Auckland) was "Euro-centric".

Her mother instilled a respect for other races and was disapproving *when anyone voiced prejudice. One of Mitzi's earliest memories is of visiting Auckland and reading an inscription on a monument which referred to the "friendly Maoris". Her mother commented, "Well they may be friendly to us, but they sound like traitors to me."*

*While studying for her Masters degree in English at Auckland University, Mitzi joined the Student Christian Movement. It was the most important influence in shaping her thinking about race, gender, peace and justice issues.*

A "sort of light" went on in Mitzi's head one night in 1970 at a meeting which was discussing the disparity between Maori and Pakeha in social statistics. A young Maori woman stood up and said she was sick of hearing about "the Maori problem" because she did not regard herself as a problem. She told the meeting that if she had a problem it was a Pakeha problem and a problem with the Pakeha system.

"Of course!" Mitzi thought. "We've been doing it all upside down!" Until that moment Mitzi Nairn had felt frustrated by all the attempts that were being made to "help" Maori.

She had become concerned about the position of Maori in New Zealand society after joining the Student Christian Movement in 1961. "It was a year after the Hunn Report was published, so everybody who was anybody was going to lectures on 'What do Maori Really Want?' and 'The Maori Problem' and how we can run better homework centres and stuff like that."

Mitzi also attended meetings of the New Zealand Council for Race Relations, which was made up of organisations such as trade unions, the PPTA and Care.

"It began to process the Hunn Report and you could feel the dissatisfaction growing about the responses we were making. Looking back at the Hunn Report now I can see all the statistics of institutional racism but we didn't have that vocabulary. Our analysis was in terms of blaming victims, really. So the solutions to what the Hunn Report showed were for Maori to try harder and catch up and we as Pakeha people of goodwill must help them more. It was a misconception of what the problem was.

"They used to discuss things like progress through after-school homework centres and all that sort of helpy stuff.

"Soon it became clear that, despite all the helping and trying harder, there was more disparity in the later sixties than there had been in the Hunn Report statistics. That was when it became clear there was something we weren't processing."

Towards the end of the sixties, new activist groups like Nga Tamatoa, the Maori Organisation on Human Rights, the Polynesian Panther Party and Black Unity began to appear. In the early seventies there was a watershed in the movement when a report was published by a work group set up by the Race Relations Council. The Nelson Action Committee had researched in the courts and prepared a document called *Maori Participation in Pakeha Justice*. "For the first time it looked at the possibility of a systematised disadvantage/advantage that had never been visible before.

"That was about the time that the word racism was beginning to be used. It was coming across from the black analysis in the United States but also got quite an indigenous flavour here."

At that time it was very difficult to talk about racism in New Zealand. Mitzi says New Zealanders left school believing that this country had the best race relations in the world. "We didn't know it was a belief. We thought it was a piece of knowledge we knew. So to have that exposed as just an opinion we held, which had no data to back it up, was quite dramatic intellectually. It affects who you are, a disclosure like that."

Mitzi and her colleagues struck defensiveness and aggressive hostility when they raised the issue. "People had strong vested interests in that cluster of myths. Tim McCreanor in his research talks about 'the standard story', which is something that everybody knows or everybody accepts. So if you are telling the standard story you never have to justify it or give evidence that supports it.

"If you want to tell an alternative story you don't just have to explain it once. You have to give it on every occasion, in every event. Looking back I see that's why the seventies were so tiring; because when you are challenging an entrenched standard story there is this merciless requirement to argue the case."

In the mid-seventies Mitzi Nairn and some other like-minded Pakeha set up a group called Auckland Committee on Racism and Discrimination. She says they had a strong base of skills in research and statistics and their purpose was to understand the new analysis and to test it out. Broadly, the analysis was that the situation was not the fault of the victims but the result of institutional racism. The members also committed themselves to putting the issue on the top of their agendas, which Mitzi says sounds crudely simple but actually made them deal with it. They met once a week for about 10 years.

ACORD broke new ground in the area of racial discrimination. They made two enquiries into the treatment of children in state welfare custody. They reported on team policing and the South Auckland taskforce. Other issues were overstayers, interpreters in hospitals and medical education.

"All our partner groups we worked in coalition with, like Nga Tamatoa, said, 'Please don't come and clutter up our organisations as Pakeha hangers-on. Please go and deal to your own.' So that was what the thing was about – dealing to our own. Some of the people in ACORD are still networked and in the same work."

It was through ACORD that Mitzi moved into education. The members found their high profile as an action group prompted people to ask them to address meetings, or Rotary luncheons, or take a session with a staff training unit. ACORD had deliberately chosen to project an abrasive style to the public and it was decided that a group with a low public profile was needed to carry out the education work.

"New Perspectives on Race was formed by a coalition from ACORD, Nga Tamatoa, Polynesian Panther Party and one or two other community groups. It turned out that I was available to do a lot of that work and although it frightened me silly, I turned out in the end to have quite an aptitude for it." Mitzi has been holding workshops for Pakeha on Treaty, race and justice issues ever since.

The Programme On Racism was set up by the National Council of Churches in 1982, a year after the Springbok tour, "in growing awareness that apartheid in South Africa is not the only manifestation of racism." Mitzi joined them a year later.

They monitor changes in the member churches, offer resources and training and run education and consultancy workshops for church and society. Typical topics for workshops are Te Tiriti o Waitangi, Introduction to Racism, Bicultural First Steps, Racism and Ministry: Pastoral Skills, Decolonisation, Treaty Issues for Professional Counsellors, Honourable Kawanatanga: Changes and Challenges.

It was tough work at first. "If you went into a room full of people and said 'I think there is such a thing as racism, and I think it happens in New Zealand' you didn't have to say anything else all morning because they just yelled at you for about two hours. Times have changed. We have put the vocab on the map."

However, the vocabulary is constantly changing too. In the seventies Mitzi and her colleagues were using words like pluralism and multiculturalism and manuhiri. Now the word tauiwi is more common than manuhiri, although Mitzi believes that too is a faulty word. She says the educators often change their technical language because it is co-opted by people in power and watered down.

"So we have to do what the young do and keep on making up new words. And we've been quite resistant to writing down the working theory of the movement – partly because we need to keep changing it and when you put it in print it sets in concrete, in ways which aren't fair. There is also the question of ownership of knowledge."

Mitzi says race issues are more up front than they were when she began. "There are more people willing to talk about it or having to talk about it unwillingly. I think people get confused about the fact that the hostility is now more on the surface and say that race relations have got worse. I would say race relations are about how they've always been but the hostility is less underground and so is the support."

Maori sovereignty is an important issue for Mitzi and for many of the people who attend her workshops. Once again she is concerned that "sovereignty" is not the best of words. "The more work I do on sovereignty the vaguer it gets. If you ask people what it means, it has very wide usage. It is everything from kings and queens and 'Off with his head!' down to something a constitutional lawyer might get pretty technical about."

She prefers to refer back to the Declaration of Independence and the Treaty of Waitangi, to look at tino rangatiratanga and kawanatanga and their relationship. "I think we could develop some agreed meanings for some of those things based on those documents."

Some aspects of sovereignty she finds "quite technical and dodgy". These are the aspects which have nothing to do with monarchs or sovereigns but are related to the international standing of a nation state to control its territories and its rights to take care of its citizens in another country.

"One of the things I see as dangerous and needing to be worked out carefully is how you maintain your international standing while you negotiate your constitutional change because you could become vulnerable. When the people of Chile elected Allende they did not think that outsiders would come in and assassinate him and undermine what they believed to be a political change through the ballot box.

"When a state becomes marginal in its legitimacy it is easy for external operators to move in on it 'for its own good'. I mean, the last thing we want is a UN peace-keeping force here which we could have if we did it stupidly or the Americans were 'helping' us. We don't need that."

Mitzi says constitutional transitions require careful attention to the international legitimacy of the state. She says if you want to make radical change then you must also maintain legitimacy along with the continuity of the state and its legislature. This has financial implications, too, "around vulnerability, trust and confidence and all those things. You don't want to revalue down to zero and have your share price index fall."

After such sobering thoughts Mitzi proceeds to talk about her desire for constitutional change. Going back to the word sovereignty, she says it has an aspect which relates to the rights of citizens or groups of citizens within the state. "If the state is not a republic but a monarchy then citizens are not citizens but subjects. This is one of the key differences. To be a subject of a king means to be a vassal or an underling or piece of property or down further in some chain of command. This makes the word citizen more appealing to me. The more I read about it the more attractive the idea of a republic becomes."

Mitzi believes New Zealanders need to have a long period of discussion about such things. She sees the need for dialogue on what is meant by sovereignty, rangatiratanga, kawanatanga, monarchy and republic and how they could work here.

"I think there is some work to be done among both parties. The kawanatanga side have work to do just as Maori do. Maori show more signs of getting on with it than Pakeha. We need a standing conference or standing forum on constitutional relationships."

Although the government has made it quite clear that Maori sovereignty cannot be discussed, Mitzi doubts that. She believes that as soon as the government denies it is on the agenda, it is actually on the agenda.

"I expect some wariness around those questions. And I think that's responsible. When I'm out demonstrating I'm not this reasonable. But there are times to be simple and wave simple placards and there are times to look at how things need to happen and I think it would be irresponsible to throw things open in dangerous ways. I think people like Bolger and Doug Graham are in positions where they do have to exercise some of that caution even if I see it as a rearguard action or a temporary thing."

The Declaration of Independence is pivotal to Mitzi Nairn's view of Maori sovereignty. "It has been one of the best-kept historical secrets. People in our workshops are often excited when they see it, and rightly so, because until you do it is really hard to understand the Treaty of Waitangi – particularly the Maori text."

The Maori text of the Treaty of Waitangi is the primary one used during her workshops. "We are more impressed by the Maori text. It's the one that has ninety per cent of the signatures on it, including both parties."

The first two articles of the Declaration of Independence read as follows:

> 1. We the hereditary chiefs and heads of the tribes of the Northern parts of New Zealand, being assembled at Waitangi, in the Bay of Islands, on this 28th day of October, 1835, declare the Independence (Rangatiratanga) of our country, which is hereby constituted and declared to be an Independent State, under the designation of the United Tribes of New Zealand.
>
> 2. All sovereign power and authority within the territories of the united tribes of New Zealand is hereby declared to reside entirely and exclusively in the hereditary chiefs and heads of tribes in their collective capacity, who also declare that they will not permit any legislative authority (wakarite ture) separate from themselves in their elective capacity to exist, nor any function of government (kawanatanga) to be exercised within the said territories, unless by persons appointed by them in Congress assembled.

"To any historical linguist it's fascinating to have two documents about the same subject within five years of each other," Mitzi says. "So it's an absolute gift in terms of what was understood and what those words meant, particularly when the translation of the Declaration was from Maori to English. 'Kawanatanga' is translated as 'the function of government' (under the direction of the rangatira). 'Rangatiratanga' is 'Independence'."

She says it seems fairly clear that the Maori of the north, when negotiating the Treaty, had a very good understanding of their own sovereignty and did not intend to give it up. At the most they may have seen the Treaty as a document of a protectorate relationship with Britain. She says they would not have signed it unless they saw it as confirming their sovereignty.

Most people attending Treaty workshops change their thinking once they have examined the information. "It's nobody's fault they don't know this stuff. It just wasn't taught. And it hasn't been around in any form you could pick up and read. The revisionist historians didn't start publishing until the seventies.

"Once people realise that they are not bad people for not knowing this stuff that had been hidden from them, it frees them to learn things. And they say, 'This affects what I've always understood. I was taught wrong things. I was allowed to make wrong assumptions.'"

Mitzi views the Treaty as a basic statement of intention which is capable of expansion and interpretation. "We didn't start working together on the Treaty when we should have in the 1840s and '50s." However, she believes it is not too late to work out what it means in practice.

"What I hear is a call to set up some kind of place where that charter of intention can be fleshed out and earthed in the realities of the present day and the future. Now I think that is perfectly feasible. I think we are a bit short on political will at the moment but I don't see it as impossible."

When she is discussing Maori sovereignty, Mitzi Nairn has a fresh perspective on the Treaty which occurred to her when she was reading the Declaration of Independence. Until now she says everyone has been too Anglo-centric in their understanding of the meaning of "kawana", a transliteration of "governor".

"There are a lot of clues which suggest that the missionaries had the American system in their minds when they translated the Declaration out of Maori into English. The Declaration uses words like in 'congress assembled' which is not from the British system. It's American."

In the past, historians have often assumed that Maori understood the word "kawana" in relation to their biblical teachings. "God had rangatiratanga and Pontius Pilate had kawanatanga – which is quite helpful – but I also think we need to look at the fact that there was interest at the time in the American political system and 'governor' is a word from that system as is 'congress'."

In America the concept of "governor" was undergoing some rapid changes. It had moved from referring to the British military governor, who ran the American colony prior to independence, to a new person who was elected to head the state legislatures.

"It seems to me we should explore some of that American development of the word. By 1840 the American constitution was already 60 years old and the role of their states and state governors may well have been part of the discussion here in New Zealand. There may be the thought that the governors, as heads of states, were like rangatira of iwi. And it was a federal system. We're not thinking of a central, up and down system, we're thinking of federation and congress."

If the missionaries were thinking of the American system, then Mitzi says Pakeha would have been another tribe represented by Congress. In 1840 there were only about three thousand people in the "Pakeha tribe" and Maori did not realise that so many more would come later.

This is one of the many aspects of the Treaty Mitzi would like to see discussed at a constitutional forum. "How the two parties to the Treaty –

being of different sizes and different historical backgrounds – how that would be worked out in practical terms so that the voices would have a balance and fairness about them.

"I come from a long cultural tradition that if you make an agreement you should stick to it or negotiate a change. It's a matter of good faith. As Jane Kelsey puts it, 'It's a matter of honour.' It's also a simple matter of justice and a solid question of peace – of having a stable, open society. I don't think you can oppress people and rely on their goodwill and peacefulness forever.

"I'm reluctant to use those arguments because I pick up a lot of fear in the system at the moment and the last thing we want to do is freak ourselves out by being fearful about this. We have been very fortunate in the amount of patience and self-control that Maori groups have shown.

"I think the Whanganui occupation was a recent example, where there was some interesting brinkmanship but it was also a very dignified withdrawal. That's very creative stuff. We've got a long history of that kind of pushing. Unless those margins and boundaries are pushed most of us will just sit on our dog houses like Snoopy, feeling reprieved and not doing anything."

The media does not reflect the fact that many Pakeha support demands for Maori sovereignty. Mitzi says it is not for want of press releases. Many groups try to make comments but cannot get newspapers to print them. In frustration, Pakeha churches in Whanganui finally bought advertising space to show their support for the Moutoa Gardens occupation.

"It doesn't fit the way news is structured in terms of conflict and fear. It un-simplifies it if people turn up on the wrong side saying 'we're not scared'."

While the dialogue Mitzi seeks on constitutional change would be a slow process, she is pleased to see some organisations taking immediate steps to share power. She says even if these models are not quite right it is enormously important to have "little models being test driven" because for most people the most difficult thing is making the first change.

"Groups like Women's Refuge and Rape Crisis have both pioneered some parallel development. Then there is the work the Anglican and Methodist churches have done. All those are brave. They are not perfect but are showing us that they have faced some crucial questions.

"What the Methodists have done is try to balance numbers in their central decision-making process so that the voices are equal, without swamping the small Taha Maori with the demands of the large Taha

Pakeha. The Anglican revision of their constitution is quite significant also because it shows that you can amend a Westminster system quite drastically and not immediately go down the gurgler. It is not business as usual, but it is still business."

Mitzi says there are recurring questions asked by Pakeha at workshops.

• What about the Moriori? Weren't the Maori colonists too? ("That's a myth," says Mitzi. "The Moriori were a tribe of similar Polynesian stock inhabiting the Chatham Islands.")

• Wasn't traditional Maori society elitist? ("My guess is that there was a lot of variation from tribe to tribe. Even today patterns differ between marae. Anyway, modern concepts of democracy are also new to Pakeha. Maoridom would not have stood still at 1840.")

• Maori seem to want separate development. Isn't that apartheid? ("South Africa's apartheid system is not the same thing as separate development. Separate development is related to autonomy, self-determination and other positive ways in which the aspirations of peoples, to control their own lives on their own terms, are expressed.")

• Why can't we just all be New Zealanders? ("We began as two peoples, agreeing to share one country, one nation, for our mutual benefit. Since then, the Treaty of Waitangi has been broken by one party which subsequently became more numerous and more powerful. The name of New Zealand belongs to that group.")

Mitzi says Maori are not simply a minority in a democracy; they are tangata whenua who have rangatiratanga in their own land. "You have to have some kind of bilateral joint nation – two nations/one nation – or you put the Crown under rangatiratanga which would be difficult to negotiate, although not impossible."

If Pakeha really want all New Zealanders to work together as one for the country, Mitzi says, it could be solved by everyone being run by tino rangatiratanga.

"That would be a more inclusive system than the way we are now because independence of action of tribal units is one of the givens of a Maori political structure – in a way that caring for minorities isn't actually a very strong given in the structure we have now. Under rangatiratanga, Pakeha would have as good provision as they have at present."

A frequent Pakeha criticism of Maori is that Maori are so divided that they are often worse to each other than anyone else is to them. The government and many other groups complain that there is not "one

Maori voice". It can be an excuse to do nothing.

Mitzi has two answers to that. Firstly she says that the strength of Maoridom is in difference. Iwi are separate groups with different kawa. "You can see when a point of contention comes up at the marae, all these old people kind of come to life and animate – and off they go. Dispute and contention are part of the cultural lifeblood. If you iron those things out I don't think you'd have the iwi any more."

Secondly she argues that division is also the result of oppression. "The whole of colonial history is one of oppression and denigration of indigenous peoples. All oppressed groups transmit the violence that they have experienced and it kind of rebounds among them. It is also safer to hit each other than to hit the oppressor who holds all the power. And often the oppressor will not enforce the same rules of peacefulness and kindness among oppressed peoples that it requires for its own citizens."

When Mitzi is asked about the role of Maori activists she smiles with enthusiasm. "Bless the activists! We owe them a huge debt. If there weren't people willing to stick their necks out and say things that sound preposterous, eventually everything would come home to roost and we would be totally unprepared for the consequences of past history. They are preparing us and giving us time to change. Good on them!"

## KEVIN SMITH

*"There are limits to human rights. The need to protect the environment really can override indigenous people's rights at times."*

**K**evin Smith is Conservation Director for the Royal Forest and Bird Protection Society. His position has brought him into conflict with iwi as he advocates protection of native forests and wildlife. However, he will not back down when he believes an important principle is at stake. As he puts it: *"There was no Treaty struck with the plants and animals of New Zealand."*

Born in 1953 in the King Country, a third generation New Zealander, he spent most of his childhood at Owhango on the banks of the Whakapapa River. His father was a bushman who had a good relationship with local Maori.

He is of mainly British extraction and regards himself as "a Pakeha through and through" despite the fact that his mother's father, born in Fiordland in 1900, was part Maori. "It's just a historical curiosity to me because I was raised as Pakeha and my three children are all blond-haired and blue-eyed types and so am I."

Kevin gained a BSc (Hons) from Canterbury University in 1972. He was a self-employed possum trapper, meat shooter and contract ecologist, living for 14 years in South Westland. He took up his present position in 1989.

Two memories from Kevin Smith's childhood have helped shape his destiny. The first was watching his father bulldoze a track through a scenic reserve. Thirteen-year-old Kevin saw beauty ahead of the bulldozer and wreckage behind and, to make matters worse, access to a favourite hidden lakelet was opened up. "I just saw how stupid and unnecessary that destruction was and how official approvals for the road were so casually given. That was when I wrote my first essay on the topic."

He was left with another lasting impression by Tuwharetoa's decision to afforest the surrounds of Lake Rotoaira. "It's a Tuwharetoa-owned lake with Mt Tongariro above it and Pihanga on the other side. My father recounted to me how there was considerable debate among Tuwharetoa about whether they should do that.

"Some of the older women were extremely upset that they were going to lose this magnificent open landscape and tussock stretching up from the lake to the mountain but the commercial imperative won out and, of course, that lake's now surrounded by radiata pine stretching up onto the slopes of Tongariro, which I find disturbingly intrusive."

What Kevin saw was two strands of Maoridom – those who had affinity and attachment to the land and wanted to retain its natural values and those who wanted to provide themselves with an economic future.

"The experience is familiar to me – the voices for conservation were outnumbered by the voices for development. And development won out with no concessions to nature in that case at all. I was also aware of what had happened to other Maori land. Like anyone else's land there, it was trashed. The Tuwharetoa did gift the central core of Tongariro National Park, but all the lowland forest they had within their rohe was trashed. Their totara resource was logged and much of it wasted and squandered, as happened everywhere."

This is the key to his approach – that Maori are no better and no worse than anyone else when it comes to the environment. And if sovereignty is being debated, Maori cannot be trusted, any more than Pakeha can, to preserve New Zealand's natural world.

In the seventies Kevin found himself on the West Coast of the South Island doing what he really wanted to do – working to save forests. He made his living trapping possums and deer shooting and in his spare time helped the Native Forest Action Council with its campaigns. It involved working with Maori in South Westland and he still cherishes a bone carving given to him by Keri Hulme for his efforts in protecting their forests.

He says he had begun to notice a great diversity in the way Maori approached environmental issues. "From individuals, hapu and iwi who are very concerned about the environment to others who are as greedy and development-minded and as callous and brutal towards nature as anyone in non-Maori society."

One of the aspects of traditional kaitiakitanga that impresses Kevin is the way Maori cared for their marine and fresh water resources and the way they still fight for them today. "That has been a strong ethic. And their attempts to protect their reefs, eel fisheries or whitebait fisheries have been frustrated so often by others who wish to exploit the resource."

He reasons that Maori people, having come from island-based societies where the only hope of survival was to care for the reef, have a long-established conservation ethic for fisheries. "Maori did have strong phobias about contamination of water with human wastes; to protect the quality of water in their lagoon and the quality of their marine food sources. However, when they encountered the forests and the amazing bird life of New Zealand, they were as much out of sync with it as we are.

"It was inevitable when humans came to New Zealand that the impact would be horrendous and it was much, much greater than a lot of people nowadays are prepared to admit. As the wave of Polynesian migration crossed the Pacific, a huge wave of extinctions followed behind them. An estimated 2000 to 3000 species of birds became extinct."

He says about 35 bird species had been pushed to extinction by the time Europeans arrived in New Zealand. Another 10 or so have become extinct since then. The birds disappeared because of the Polynesian rat, the kiore, and the Polynesian dog, the kuri, and because early Maori killed the birds as food and cleared their forest habitat.

"Maori cleared 30 to 40 per cent of the forest. The big clearances were on the eastern side of the South Island – the forests that were most susceptible to fire – and the Bay of Plenty, central North Island and Northland."

Kevin acknowledges some effective Maori conservation practices such as the traditional method for harvesting flax. The leaves were taken off in a way that did not kill the plant. However, he is highly critical of the management of birds like the kereru by Maori in the past and the present.

"Some kaumatua in Northland, where the kereru is facing extinction, see the killing and poaching of kereru as a running joke against Pakeha. Folk like Kevin Prime, an elder of Ngati Hine, who has spoken out against it, are pretty much a lone voice."

To his mind, Maori place conservation lower on the agenda than other issues such as reasserting the culture and resolving grievances. "While they are dealing with that, the time for nature is running out so rapidly and our forests and wildlife are collapsing. By the time Maoridom is able to give conservation its just attention, they will have lost so much that is of value to them as well as the wider community."

His commitment is so strong that he believes New Zealanders must safeguard the future of native plants and animals above their own futures where they can. This is the philosophy which underpins Forest and Bird's attitude to land claims.

"For those Maori who want land for land, the problem is that most of the lands remaining in public ownership in New Zealand are the conservation lands. And they only remain largely because of the determination of people and organisations, like Forest and Bird and Federated Mountain Clubs, over the years to resist successive waves of privatisation and development which has seen virtually all the lowlands and developable land in New Zealand freeholded.

"I see Doug Graham sitting there, casting around trying to find some land to resolve the raupatu claims or Ngai Tahu claim. And he can't find any until he looks up to the hills and says 'Thank God for the greenies'."

Kevin says New Zealand business, agriculture and forestry have built up enormous wealth based on the fertile lowlands. "Much of that should have been used for resolution of the claims or should have remained in Maori ownership to start with."

In many areas only the conservation lands are left. "You can't get an economic return from them unless you exploit them in a way that compromises their protection. So it is a huge injustice to nature, a huge injustice to the conservation public, to focus on them."

Forest and Bird is "exceptionally grateful" to Tainui. Kevin says no one could dispute the justice of Tainui's claim and recognises how hard it must have been for the tribe to be told that the conservation lands were not available for their settlement, even though those lands had been confiscated from them.

"To agree to those conservation lands remaining in public ownership was an incredibly important gesture by the Tainui. They got some other lands but, of course, much of the land that should have been theirs is now the dairy farms and the stud farms of the Waikato.

"It's an injustice that the Treaty of Waitangi Tribunal Act puts private land out of bounds for Tribunal recommendations. On a 'willing seller' basis the Crown should be purchasing land on the open market for use in the settlement of claims."

Other alternatives for settling land claims he suggests are the resources owned by State Owned Enterprises, pine forests and native timber production forests on the West Coast of the South Island. Natural resources such as geothermal energy and pounamu should also be available for Maori claimants, according to Kevin. He says the government's resistance to some of the claims for natural resources is more a desire to hold on to an economic resource than any public interest.

In his view there are a number of tribes who have every right to claim the return of conservation lands to Maori ownership. Tuhoe and Taranaki are examples. However, he wants them to follow Tainui's lead and forego their property rights in a gesture to help protect the natural world.

Forest and Bird agrees that Maori should be consulted in the management of such lands, that they should have Maori values recognised in the management. "As in the Tainui settlement. They will now have a position, as of right, on the Waikato Conservation Board. I think that can occur elsewhere."

The conservation lobby has no objection to the transfer of title to urupa or sacred sites. Kevin Smith says "maybe" he would also agree to the government's proposal to return some particular Maori sites of special significance. However, this is where he starts to have doubts.

"I would suggest to Maoridom that conservation lands are a huge liability. The forests are collapsing and degrading under the impact of pests and that's the real challenge; to see that anything remains, the survival of the natural world.

"Mt Taranaki is important to Taranaki Maori but it is also cherished and loved by the wider community as well. We both love the same lands and we both identify with them, so there is an overlap of interest there. I believe that joint interest can be best expressed through the Crown retaining the ownership and management but through Maori participation and consultation in management.

"Allocating conservation lands to Maori is not going to do anything to lift the economic status of Maori. It's not going to do anything to address their over-representation in all the unfortunate social and economic statistics, whether it's prisons or mental hospitals. It isn't really going to assist Maoridom to up its standard of education or economic well-being. And yet the pressures will be on those lands, if they become their resource, to exploit them in that way. And Maori are just as vulnerable to those pressures as anyone else."

Any Maori control over conservation lands is something Kevin Smith is prepared to accept in a limited way only. He says Maori should most definitely have the final say in the conservation estate over the interpretation of their history, management of their urupa or some of their most sacred sites, although the Department of Conservation should decide the level of any customary use of plants and animals.

Beyond that he sees firm boundaries. "If it extends on to become sovereign control of areas, then what comes first? It always must be subject to the Resource Management Act and sustainable management provisions of that; also the Conservation Act and the Wildlife Act, so that there are restraints on the sovereignty of anybody."

Forest and Bird has found itself in a see-saw relationship with Maori. One minute they are working co-operatively on a joint initiative, the next they are locked in a bitter battle over principles. For instance, Kevin is proud of their relationship with Ngai Tahu in establishing Te Waipounamu South West World Heritage area and their assistance to the Whanganui Maori Trust Board in the campaign to restore water to the Whanganui River.

When it comes to confrontation with Maori the "most spectacular" was the disagreement with Ngati Porou over the East Coast forestry project. The government put up a subsidy to establish commercial pine plantations as part of a soil conservation programme. Ngati Porou sought a joint venture with Tasman Forestry to establish 50,000 hectares of pine forest around Ruatoria and the row with environmentalists erupted.

Forest and Bird said the forest would require clearing of tall kanuka shrub lands and they had struck an accord with Tasman, and other major forestry companies, that they would not clear such areas for pine plantations. Kevin says the whole deal failed because the government was inflexible about its subsidies. He is not proud of the outcome because Ngati Porou have ended up with nothing and they saw Forest and Bird's actions as trampling on their rights to do what they wanted with their land.

Kevin has had another head-on argument with the Maori owners of Waitutu Forest to prevent any logging there. Once again Kevin says he can identify with the Maori grievance. "They did have the productive farm land of the Southland plains whipped out from under their noses and settled by Europeans. They were given a bit of useless bush in the back of beyond as an economic alternative for the landless natives at the turn of the century and now all their attempts to turn a dollar out of that forest have been frustrated.

"However, on an international scale it's one of the most important blocks of remaining natural forest anywhere in the world so they have no right to destroy that forest. They say they would rather not do it, but they would do it!"

Kevin says this helps to explain his general opposition "to Maori sovereignty, Maori control, joint management, veto rights or decision-making rights" over publicly owned conservation areas.

"One thing I find difficult is the liberal white view that it's culturally unsafe to have these stoushes with Maoridom. I find that a very patronising approach. I am often criticised for being prepared to get up and argue the toss with Maori. I find Maoridom enjoys a good argument and are very good at it in the theatre of the marae and the cut and thrust of the debate there. And I don't believe that we will make any real progress unless we are prepared to have open and honest debates."

He acknowledges that the attitude of some elements in the conservation lobby is racist. A proportion of his own members would be "fervent supporters of the One New Zealand Foundation" and he gets congratulatory letters from them when he says something that coincides with their views. Knowing this, Kevin is very conscious that Forest and Bird must guard against over-reaction. "We do have to moderate our language. I have a responsibility in my position not to wind people up in a way that can be destructive.

"Equally some of our members find it difficult to be described by some Maori as eco-Nazis. I would offer the same counsel to those in Maori activism. Activism is important and healthy and the only way to get things changed. But you have to moderate the methods you use, otherwise you end up creating such bitter and permanent divisions between people that you can never bridge them."

Kevin Smith is worried about the implications of Whanganui Maori asserting sovereignty in their rohe. Forest and Bird has applied for a water conservation order for the Whanganui River but the society was not invited to participate when the Minister of Conservation set up a committee of iwi there to advise on the issue.

"One concern I have about heading down the sovereignty approach is this exclusivity of an iwi committee which doesn't end up interacting with other interests. If there is to be a resolution to Whanganui's problems, for example, it has to involve interaction with Forest and Bird, Ruapehu

District Council and Federated Farmers. I'd be worried if we didn't end up working together by going down the sovereignty line."

For the most part Kevin sees the Resource Management Act as meeting Maori needs because it gives tangata whenua a special right to be recognised and consulted about their values, and for those values to be protected. He admits the Act has imperfections, citing the Cook Strait fast ferry decision as one which "tramples on Maori rights and destroys the environment". However, the answer, as he sees it, is not to toss the Act aside but to make it more effective.

He asserts that the Crown's ownership of reserves is largely justified, saying there are limits to human rights and the need to protect the environment can override indigenous people's rights at times.

The idea that Maori could be granted some sort of symbolic ownership of the land does not meet his favour either. He says title and ownership of land mean power and control, so constraints on that are often ineffective when you try to enforce them.

He cites as an example the Maori ownership of the Titi Islands and the beneficial islands around Stewart Island which are jointly managed with the Crown. Kevin claims that harvesting mutton birds has caused damage to the natural ecology of the islands. "What they are driven by is the commercial imperative for the mutton bird harvest rather than the spiritual, cultural and natural protection of the islands.

"Everyone should lose sovereignty in this area." He points to an increasing amount of legislation which restricts landowners. They can no longer clearfell their forests or cut down native trees without restriction. They are not free to drain wetlands and do what they like with waterways.

Tino rangatiratanga rather than sovereignty is what Kevin sees, in part, being recognised in the conservation sector. He says tino rangatiratanga means Maori being represented, as of right, on the Conservation Authority. It means iwi being consulted about management strategies in DOC. "The Conservation Act itself states that the department must give effect to the principles of the Treaty. That is not meeting the demands for sovereignty but it is meeting tino rangatiratanga."

He draws the line at any suggestion of equal partners managing the conservation estate because he foresees conflicting aspirations for the land. "Protection so often conflicts either with the desire to make money out of it from tourism, to build hydro stations, to make money out of water, to harvest totara or kauri for various purposes or to kill native birds. So I don't see 50/50 arrangements being workable.

"It's a recipe for conflict. The wider community would be largely excluded from that decision-making arrangement."

Kevin says part of the problem for him in relating to Maori over Treaty settlements has been their unwillingness to talk directly to groups like Forest and Bird. Maori say their business is with the Crown and no one else. "But it is very difficult for us because we are most definitely going to talk to the Crown. So our views get filtered through to Maori by them and Maori views get filtered back to us and it's a real recipe for misunderstanding."

Another factor which polarises public opinion on Maori issues is the media, in Kevin's view. He noticed what he calls "glaring double standards" in the "hysterical response" to the Moutoa Gardens occupation.

"No one's been particularly concerned about Pakeha who occupy bits of land with their baches and shacks, that have occupied the Queen's chain or public reserves around the country, until Maori started making a conspicuous point of it. Then suddenly occupation was a huge threat to the whole fabric of New Zealand society. Yet our public lands are littered with people occupying them illegally."

Kevin congratulates Doug Graham and Jim Bolger for embarking on proposals for settling claims. However, the government's decision to confine claims to a capped fiscal envelope has worried the environmental lobby because it puts greater pressure on the conservation lands as a way to accommodate Maori demands.

"We do want the resolution of claims. We want Maori to lift their economic and social standing in the community so that they are able to provide better educational opportunities for their children. The focus on conservation lands is unfortunate because it is not going to help Maori lift their economic status at all. In fact, these lands are a liability because of the huge burden to manage them with pest control and to rescue threatened species.

"I also hear what Maori are saying – that economic resourcing is not the only issue. They want their mana recognised, their tino rangatiratanga, their special status recognised and their chieftainship over their taonga. So I accept that.

"The greatest challenge is to meet Maoridom's concerns and needs while not threatening conservation values or alienating the wider public from those natural lands which the public love and cherish as well."

No matter what he says about these issues, Kevin finds himself offending people. "Some will see what I am saying as capitulating to

Maori and others will see it as trampling all over them – and Forest and Bird will get resignations on both sides. It's tempting for us to pull our heads in and not participate in the debate. But the issue is too important and we are too centrally placed in the conservation community. We have fifty-six branches all around the country so we are also in a good position to communicate with iwi."

Fortunately, for a man in his position, Kevin does not mind a robust debate and he envisages a positive future for Maori and Pakeha together.

"Forest and Bird are an indigenous group with firm principles. We're not really pushing our self-interest. Our objective is one we hope Maori would share – I think they do – which is to ensure that New Zealand's native plants and animals survive here."

## KEN DOUGLAS

*"The process of colonisation was a process of exploitation and theft. That's in its politest sense. There was raping and pillaging and murder and all those sorts of things. So those historical wrongs have to be put right."*

**B**orn in 1935 to working class parents, Ken Douglas is a fourth generation New Zealander of Gaelic and English ancestry. He has lived all his life in Wellington. During the war Ken's parents split up so he was raised largely by his grandmother. He attended Wellington College from 1949 to '53. Nowadays he has four children of his own and seven grandchildren who are all part Maori.

Ken Douglas began his trade union career in 1959 as an organiser for the Wellington Drivers' Union. He later became Secretary/Treasurer of the New Zealand Federation of Labour and in 1987 took up his present position as President of the New Zealand Council of Trade Unions. He joined the Communist Party in 1960 and six years later left to help form the Socialist Unity Party.

He is a softly spoken man respected for his intellect and cool headedness in union disputes.

He believes that everyone, including Maori, should see themselves as citizens of the world, not citizens of particular countries. So he reflects

***an internationalist attitude to indigenous people and their struggles just as he does to workers and workers' problems.***

About a quarter of the children in Ken Douglas's primary school in the working class suburb of Northland were Maori but he says kids were kids and it wasn't a big deal in those days. His family were "quite political in a labour sense" so they were conscious of racism. "I remember my grandfather talking about the racism against the Irish, how they were the butt of jokes and so on. He said when the Irish get established it will be somebody else. He said it will probably be Pacific Islanders and Maoris."

As a teenager Ken began to be more aware of the differences between Maori and Pakeha as he mixed with Maori pupils who had come to board at Wellington College. One thing that stands out in his memory is a school mate, Len Timoana, who sat School Certificate in the same year as he did. Len took Maori as a subject and was the only student in Wellington in 1952 who did so. "He and I were good friends so I didn't think there was anything odd about it. The thing that surprised me was that he was the only one taking School Cert Maori."

A number of Ken's schoolmates were fluent speakers and active in the affairs of their tribes. A close friend was the elder son of Frank Winter, the chairman of the Ngai Tahu Trust Board.

When Ken left school and was playing rugby for College Old Boys he met a young Maori footballer who was an electrical apprentice from Waitara. "He was living in an old doss house at the top of Willis Street. I gave him a ride home and found out where he was living and said 'You can't live in a place like this.' So he came and lived with us for about two years."

That was the first time Ken became conscious of what he called a "colour bar" against Maori as far as residential accommodation in Wellington was concerned. "He'd had trouble finding a flat and he'd ended up in this shocking bloody place."

In 1960, as a consequence of his involvement with the Drivers' Union and having known Frank Winter, Ken became involved with the Citizens' All Black Tour Association. The issues of that campaign developed his political awareness.

"I was really personally appalled, as many New Zealanders were, that Maoris were not allowed to go to South Africa because of the apartheid system there. We used to say that the Maori were good enough to take their rifles to North Africa but not good enough to take their rugby boots to South Africa."

It was as a result of that heightened awareness about racial discrimination in New Zealand, and racism in general, that Ken Douglas joined the Communist Party. "Because it seemed to me that racism inherently grew out of the system of capitalism. So, for my sins, my political activism actually flowed from an emotional reaction to racial discrimination rather than an intellectual knowledge about class and those sorts of things."

When Paul Robeson came to New Zealand in the early sixties, Ken was involved through the Drivers' Union with organising his activities in Wellington. Robeson sang in concerts and made speeches at union meetings. The black singer made a very powerful impression on Ken about the whole issue of racism, much more so than figures like Martin Luther King. "When you meet a person like that the memory and the emotionalism of his words cut more deeply into you than reading somebody's words or hearing them on the radio."

The Communist Party did not meet all of his expectations in the area of race relations. He says party members were a bit confused because at one time they were advocating what almost appeared to be an apartheid system, saying that certain areas of New Zealand should be set aside for Maori. The theory was based on what Marxists called the nationalities question, ". . . the idea of a nation being a people who have a common language and a common land area and have established economic relations. So it's moved past tribal society to a nation.

"They were trying to artificially, in an honest way I think, to deal with this whole issue of Maori rights in a context of what they weren't. It seems to me that at the time of colonisation Maori weren't a nation. In fact the Treaty refers to them as the United Tribes of New Zealand. So the Communist Party were coming at it from the point of view of how did you create, in the context of the post-colonial era, a concept of national sovereignty and economic independence."

While the young Ken Douglas did not always agree with the policies, he found the debate on Maori issues within the party very useful. It was the reason he had joined in the first place; to try to understand such things. Nevertheless, he was offended by the idea of separatism. "It seemed to me that you couldn't have good separatism and you couldn't have bad separatism; like you couldn't have nice apartheid. It frankly wasn't an effective solution."

Just as he did 30 years ago, Ken believes developing a Maori economy is a critical element in the whole issue of Maori sovereignty. He aligns it with the question of how workers can achieve influence in society, believing it is no good just having the right to vote if you do not have economic democracy. "Democracy is not just about voting every three years. It's about influencing the decision-making process. Economic democracy is as important as political democracy – which is really the underlying issue about Maori rights in the context of a national economy."

Ken recalls how communists were active, not just in theory, but also in organising practical support and solidarity. A major reason for that was the huge number of Maori in trade unions. For instance, in the 1940s the unions in Auckland responded to Princess Te Puea's call for solidarity at Orakei marae when a stockade was built to stop the acquisition of the land there. He says the Communist Party was a key organiser.

Philosophically, the socialists empathised with the Maori concept of social ownership of the land and the idea that tribal societies saw preservation of the land as their heritage and future. Ken Douglas says that is why socialists and progressive labour people identify with the need to protect Maori land interests and to right the wrongs of the process of colonisation.

Ken still considers himself a Marxist and retains his interest in Maori independence and Maori economic development although he left the Communist Party in 1966 and helped to form the Socialist Unity Party.

"The left movement in all its pieces – whether it be Marxist or Trotskyist or Left Labour or whatever – I think it's made a contribution to developing an understanding of exploitation in general and it's as a consequence of understanding the nature of capitalism that the nature of racism is immediately identified."

Marxism encourages Ken to analyse in a scientific way what he calls the dialectics of historical materialism, the issues of Maori exploitation and the circumstance that Maori now find themselves in. He regards history as an important element in the whole process of understanding the cause of change as opposed to the effects of change. He says the debate around the economic and sovereign rights of Maori is much sharper in 1995 than it was in 1960 because of that historical process. Another example he gives is how the "No Maoris No Tour" campaign in 1960 was a significant lead-up to the Springbok tour protests in 1981.

"So it's like a spiral of time. The issues go around, they almost come back to the same point but they are further ahead and more people are aware of them."

Recently Ken's thinking has been influenced by reading Nelson Mandela's autobiography. In it the South African leader talks about the issue of tribalism and why it is so important to the African way of life. However, Ken noted that the traditional and cultural heritage of tribes need not lock them into a timewarp. Tribalism was essentially a paternalistic society but Mandela says you cannot have the values of tribalism in today's circumstances without recognising the rights of women.

"That's been an underlying tension in Maoridom for some time, but being sort of worked through. It's saying that you don't stand still in time and ignore the realities of change. You take the good of the past and blend it with the promise of the new."

Indigenous people's rights are an internationalist issue for Ken. He says as a unionist he cannot view Maori rights in an exclusive way because the concepts of working class solidarity spread past national boundaries. On behalf of the CTU he is a member of several Asian and Pacific trade union bodies which recognise indigenous people's rights. One of them, the South Pacific Oceanic Council of Trade Unions, even offers support for indigenous independence movements.

"In New Caledonia, where the Kanak struggle became quite vicious, there were union initiatives to support the Kanaks to try and disrupt the supply of arms to the French colonial forces there. Involvement in the independence movement of another country raises the question of what you are doing about the independence of the indigenous people in your own country."

One answer to that question is the Combined Trade Unions' policy to recognise the Treaty of Waitangi. "The process of colonisation was a process of exploitation and theft. That's in its politest sense. There was raping and pillaging and murder and all those sorts of things. So those historical wrongs have to be put right.

"The Treaty is significant in the sense of what it means for modern New Zealand. It is a demonstration of an undertaking of an active partnership. And that's why the process of its recognition can only be good for New Zealand. As a workers' representative I would say that the government shows a good example of the contradictory nature of these sorts of values. On the one hand it talks about the awareness of its obligations as a partner with Maori but on the other hand denies that to workers. I don't think you can be inconsistent like that."

Within its own structure the CTU has a national runanga which provides two Maori members for the 15-member national executive. Ken says the CTU has also built a relationship with the National Maori Congress to co-operate on such issues as Maori unemployment and to press politicians for an independent Maori economy.

"Awareness in the union movement is not as high as many would like or even I would like, but the fact that it is significantly higher than it was five or ten years ago is a truth." He admits there were differences and debates about the accountability of the separate runanga structure within the CTU at first. However, he says the process of debate was as important as the issue itself and the idea is now more accepted by the membership.

One wider debate that makes him annoyed is the question about whether New Zealand should become a republic. He sees it as an example of how the political process distorts things. "It's viewed by significant sections of Maoridom that this is just a smart Pakeha trick to undermine the standing of the Treaty. Now I'm very firmly a Republican. I don't think that the British Crown plays any useful role for the New Zealand economy or the people of New Zealand.

"The continuation of our legal system being based on the Privy Council denies the progression of our own identity as a country. But I can well understand the reasons why Maori would be suspicious of that intent. The issue really should be – and why I would favour an end to the monarchy would be – that New Zealand would then be required to have a constitution. That constitution obviously should be based on the founding document of our country, which is the Treaty of Waitangi."

So how do his views on the British monarchy relate to the hereditary chiefs of Maoridom? Ken accepts that "they have a role in the context of history and the tradition of the tribes and probably a positive influence in continuing the awareness of Maori about where they came from". However, he contends that urban Maoridom is largely unrepresented by the traditional leadership so the evolution of Maori rights must address their needs.

Again he points to South Africa and how they are addressing similar problems. "That will be very instructive for us as well because it is not about maintaining privilege for a small elite. Whether it's a Maori elite or a European elite is not the issue. And of course there are contradictions within the Maori relationships between the different tribes because of the traditional way in which control over certain lands and resources was established. It was essentially by the act of possession. Now that's a contradiction – in terms of righting those historical grievances – that has got to be worked through."

The CTU leader has also been watching the debate in Maori circles over what should be the paramount structure – hapu or iwi? Differing views have been highlighted by the Tainui settlement and in his opinion it is a key issue because ownership and control are the essential elements of the evolution of a Maori economy and Maori independence. "We won't get any significant progress on the issue of sovereignty until economic independence is established."

Ken supports the idea that tangata whenua have a special status in this country, although he qualifies that by saying it is not about a status of privilege over disadvantage. He quotes the Irish revolutionary James Connelly, at the Easter Uprising of 1916 during the battle of the post office in Dublin. "He said the issue wasn't to change English masters for Irish masters, it was to get rid of masters altogether. So the evolution of a more democratic New Zealand has got to be about empowering Maori workers as much as it is about empowering Maoris."

He understands the concept that in some cases Maori feel an absolute right and a duty as kaitiaki to make decisions in certain areas. On this subject he would look at whether it was an exercise of veto or an exercise of an obligation in a partnership relationship. "In the case of say pollution of a harbour where it is about ownership and control of taonga guaranteed under the Treaty, maybe, but in terms of governance I wouldn't support the concept of some sort of veto. You don't correct an historical wrong by creating a new wrong. It's about democratic rights and individual rights for all people as well as the specific rights of the tangata whenua."

Ken interprets the Treaty as saying that the Maori people who actually had influence and control and ownership of their particular land should keep it. That was a specific right which did not mean a universal right over the whole country and Maori were not identified as a collective whole. He says Tainui has identified the way it wishes to exercise that right in 1995. What is right for Tainui might not be right for Ngai Tahu and the various tribes will need to sort those things out for themselves.

When it comes to rectifying the wrongs, he believes it has to start with the land because the land holds the mana and is what was misappropriated. However, he cannot accept Maori claims that resources, such as minerals and oil, are part of the taonga guaranteed under the Treaty. Ken would regard Maori ownership of such resources as one rule for one and another rule for another. He says natural resources belong to the state collectively.

He contends it was the lands, forests and fisheries that were specifically referred to in the Treaty, not the minerals.

"The issue of how Maori sovereignty is resolved is not just for Maori alone. I don't think you can arrive at an objective, no matter how fine or well-meaning that objective is, if the process of getting there doesn't reflect the same values and principles as the objective itself." He is referring to partnership. Partnership in working out solutions and partnership as the result. For him it does not matter if it is not resolved quickly as long as the process is under way.

In the same breath the CTU leader thinks time is running out for addressing economic discrimination. "Because there is an increased expectation among young Maori in particular that because they are clearly being disadvantaged in the whole political process and the economic system and they are on the wrong side of the bad statistics, that it's got to be put right."

Ken Douglas believes you cannot solve economic discrimination by dealing only with Treaty issues – although that may help to alleviate the problems. In Tainui's case, for instance, he says the settlement is not about handing out dollar notes. It is about creating a foundation so that Tainui can create more skills for their people and take greater control of their lives.

The Moutoa Gardens occupation in Whanganui in 1995 had Ken worried. He did not laugh at the symbolism when a head was knocked off a statue in the park because he saw it as being more dangerous than that. He calls the protest an attempt to take a short cut which resulted in a huge amount of "redneckism". He thought it was a gamble which could have sparked retaliatory violence from some "loopy" against the Maori there. While he believes Maori are entitled to feel frustration, he would focus on broadening awareness about the issues, to draw more support from the wider population for Maori demands.

He warns Maori activists about the risks of flushing out racists in New Zealand. "I think the One New Zealand Foundation – this right-wing outfit over in Tauranga, who are apparently recruiting members hand over fist – they're very scary people, I tell you. And that's what we're playing with. The Ku Klux Klan seems a long way away and those Afrikaner people who brutalised blacks in South Africa seem a long way away now. But they are the same people, the same mentality. They've got to be flushed out, but they have to be flushed out in a way that makes people aware of what the problem is. You don't do it by posing a radical black nationalism to a radical white conservatism or white racism."

From a strategic point of view he would advise activists such as Ken Mair that you have to be effective where your influence can be the greatest. Ken Mair, a former trade unionist from the PPTA, was a prominent figure in the occupation at Moutoa Gardens.

"I know Ken Mair very well and he always goes a bit far. That's the way he sees life. He would say that what he's learnt about life is that you continually step across the line in order to get the line shifted. My point would be from experience as a unionist that every strike action – and strike action does have to be taken – all that it actually does is create the conditions for another meeting. So what are we actually trying to influence? If we are trying to beat the government . . . well unless you are prepared to take arms against the government you won't beat them."

Ken's communist belief in revolution is not the classical revolution of "throwing bombs, shooting people, carting them away and executing them and imposing a new regime by force". He says terror and violence have never been the weapons of the working class. An example he gives of a revolution in New Zealand is the impact of Rogernomics in the 1980s.

"I think there has also been a radical revolution in the thinking of most New Zealanders about their awareness about the wrongs that were caused to the Maori people and there is a quiet sense of determination that those wrongs should be put to rights in the best way we can."

The CTU leader does favour civil disobedience where this is a tactic suited to the circumstances of the time but once again he says people must be careful about their objective. He finds Nelson Mandela instructive on this point. In his book Mandela describes the number of times the ANC were tempted to go just a bit further because they seemed to be getting so much support but Ken says they disciplined themselves and asked what was the objective of the particular campaign. In New Zealand he cites Te Whiti Rongomai (a pacifist chief of Parihaka) as a role model. "We've got those images of leaders in Maoridom. And that's the importance of using our history and the processes of history."

The idea of parallel Maori and Pakeha parliaments he greets with scepticism. Ken says it is not the form so much as the content that is important. "I don't think there is any answer other than one person one vote. But that doesn't mean the subjugation of the minority by the majority. That's not democracy." He expects MMP to bring improvements for Maori voters.

Ken is horrified when he hears people say that Maori are the only ones who can do anything to help Maori. "Why should they be?" he asks. "It's like women's issues. Why should just women take up the issues of women's rights? We used to have a saying in the union movement: 'White workers can never be free while Black workers are in chains.' And that's quite right."

**DON RIESTERER**

*"I think the idea of a separate Maori parliament is a knee-jerk reaction — an easy way out, like a divorce. If your marriage is breaking down it's not easy to sit down and talk the thing through and get it back together again. Perhaps that's one of our troubles in New Zealand. We dissolve partnerships too easily."*

Don Riesterer was born in Otahuhu in 1930. His father was a railway worker, so the family lived in many places until Don began secondary school in Hawera. Don's great-grandfather arrived from Germany in 1860 so he is a fourth generation New Zealander. His mother's people arrived from England a generation later.

His parents did not think of themselves as prejudiced but the family ethos was: "Don't play with the scruffy Maori kids down the end of the street, Roman Catholics are going to take over New Zealand and you don't buy Japanese stuff." Don's best mate was one of those "scruffy Maori kids" but he did not let on to his parents.

Don received a Physical Education degree from Otago University. He worked for the YMCA for 16 years but was a school teacher for most of his life. He was Deputy Principal at Opotiki College for eight years and then Principal at Tongariro High School in Turangi for six years.

*At his first school position in Rotorua he found himself teaching many Maori pupils and outside work most of his friends were Maori because he played for a predominantly Maori rugby team. "I started to realise then that there was a whole culture that I was sharing, that a lot of Pakeha weren't privy to."*

*In 1989 Don Riesterer was elected as Mayor of Opotiki and he has now served two terms in that office. He is the Vice President of the Local Government Association and chairman of the association's Maori Consultative Committee. His wife and three children are Maori.*

At 23 when Don brought his Maori wife home to meet his parents they were worried and upset. "Their major worries were what colour the children would be. I remember having a wonderful discussion with my mother about how we might have three different coloured children – one might come out dark brown, another light brown and another white. She asked how the kids would feel about that."

Don's in-laws were uneasy about their daughter marrying a non Roman Catholic, but, in time, both families accepted the marriage. More than 40 years later Don and his wife, Josie, have two sons and a daughter – all proud to be Maori – and six mokopuna.

Josie understands some Maori language but was not brought up to speak it. "She had been brought up in the era when many Maori parents did not want their children to be Maori. They could see more advantages for them down the Pakeha track. If you asked my daughter which of her parents were Maori, she used to say, 'Dad by nature and Mum by birth!'"

Don was drawn to Maori culture during his days playing rugby and indoor basketball in Rotorua. He enjoyed the companionship, team spirit and the fun they had together. Most of all he was struck by the acceptance his Maori mates had of each other – something that, he felt, was not so apparent among Pakeha.

"There was more competing with each other in the Pakeha world. In the rugby context, if someone made a mistake in your team, you said, 'Never mind, we'll be behind you' or laugh it away. Whereas in the more highly competitive Pakeha scene you often bitched about it or told the guy to get his act together. So there was a growing understanding there of the aroha between people."

When he was 40, after 16 years away from teaching (he had been Chief Executive Officer for the YMCA in Invercargill and Auckland), Don took up a job as a Phys Ed teacher at Opotiki College. He found himself, once again, among large numbers of Maori students (60 per cent of the roll was Maori) but this time new issues had developed which were not around in his early teaching days.

Don says the full employment days of the fifties and sixties were beginning to end. "The teamwork jobs; the freezing works, road construction, fencing, shearing, all those highly skilled jobs they call unskilled – you try and shear a sheep or drive a bulldozer and see how unskilled it is – all those jobs that Maori were filling, suddenly became compressed. The freezing works got more technology, the sheep numbers dropped off so there was less work around – and the losers were Maori."

Over the next 10 years Don watched how most of the problems for his pupils at school were related to the social situations of their families. Another issue he had to face was what he calls "knocking off the tall poppy" or "the tall poppy syndrome".

"'We all need to be the same.' 'Don't let anybody stand out.' That's still a major issue in many respects. I had learnt it very early on as a Phys Ed teacher. When I tried to get a young fellow who was doing some beautiful gymnastic work to demonstrate to the rest of the class, he fooled around and wouldn't do it. When I growled at him later, he said he wasn't going to show off in front of his mates. That was a learning curve for me in that he was really saying, no way was he going to stand out."

At Tongariro High School, when Don took up his principal position, he found passes in School Certificate and University Entrance way below the national average. He was not prepared to accept that the pupils – a large proportion of whom were Maori – were any different from any other New Zealand youngsters, so he set a target of two years for the school to bring itself up to the national average.

"It meant I had to talk to the staff about their perceptions and their marking of the kids. Part of the problem was that the staff were marking to what they thought was the level of the pupil, rather than getting the pupil to raise their level. And by the third year we were up to the national average.

"That showed me something. If you set targets and enable the kids to reach those goals – Maori and/or Pakeha – they'll get there. We developed the opportunity for kids to come and do their homework at school, because you couldn't do it in a house full of six kids with nowhere to sit except around the table with the TV going."

He says the big difference in New Zealand now is the question of social equity and points to the balance of Maori compared with Pakeha in the unemployment figures. "If within the home situation it's a continuous struggle to get the necessities of living, then reading and homework are going to be low priorities. It's not that you want it to happen. You don't have the energy to do it or the funds to provide what's needed to do it with. And I think we've got to do a lot more, nationally, to look at the damage our big unemployment queues still have on our communities.

"You're talking about self-respect, you're talking about mana, you're talking about expectation of where you will go and what you will do."

Don sees Maori issues from a different perspective these days, after six years as the Mayor of Opotiki. Half of his ratepayers are Maori and 48 per cent of the total population of his district council area is Maori. His administration stretches from Cape Runaway to a line midway between Whakatane and Opotiki and encompasses four iwi – Whakatohea, Te Whanau a Apanui, Ngaitai and Te Whanau a Te Ehutu.

Only one councillor is Maori and Don is disappointed about that. He says he tried very hard at the last election to get some strong Maori candidates to stand but, in the end, they did not. He hopes for more success at the next election.

In 1989 the council set up a consultative committee to work with Maori. Don believes the committee was one of the first of its kind to be set up by a local body. "I've always believed Opotiki has a wonderful opportunity of being a crucible of Maori/Pakeha relationships for the rest of the country, because of the balance of our races. It won't be long before every Pakeha in Opotiki will have a Maori mokopuna and every Maori grandparent will have a Pakeha grandson or granddaughter. The intermarriage and crossing over between the races is such that the distinction is getting less and less."

The consultative committee, which comprises three members from each of the four iwi, meets with the council every three months to discuss Maori issues. "We agreed at our very first meeting that we were only going to work on a consensus. If we didn't reach a consensus then we would go away and come back and try again. The council also agreed that it wouldn't make a decision that was going to be contrary to what the consultative committee had agreed upon. That's quite a breakthrough."

Some of the councillors tell their Mayor that they spend a lot of time talking and do not really achieve much. However, Don says recently when they rewrote their district plan to include a protocol between the council and Maori it was well received by iwi. Don believes discussion over the protocol is proving easier because of the work the council has done with the consultative committee over the years. He puts it down to the trust which has been built up.

"I believe that local government in New Zealand has to build up a sense of trust and understanding between their iwi and councils. At a national level, our Local Government Association consultative committee has said to our members that they will achieve much more if they don't just go to see Maori when they want to talk about the Resource Management Act.

"It's important if the local Maori people know you, because you have been there at the tangi of special people or at hui, or at weddings or birthday celebrations, so that you are seen as identifying with the community. Then you'll find that often the pathway is smoother when it comes to talking about the real issues of the RMA and its requirements."

The Resource Management Act is forcing local bodies into a new relationship with Maori because it requires them to have regard for Maori values and to consult with the tangata whenua. Don says many Maori are beginning to see that it gives them considerable power in local body affairs.

In his capacity as Vice President of the Local Government Association, Don pointed out a need to involve Maori more in the New Zealand organisation as well as in his own Opotiki area. The association asked him to set up the national consultative committee.

"We called for nominations of Maori elected members, and for nominations from Maori staff, and selected them from around the country – not on a tribal basis but on a local government basis. We have eight Maori men and women and two staff people. So far we have met three times and have really just dealt with some guidelines to councils. That's all we've done. But we are getting to know each other and getting a feel for some of the issues."

He says it is a really strong committee and he expects them to come up with some interesting policy. "The guidelines so far have followed pretty closely the views of the Commissioner for the Environment, Helen Hughes. They suggest lots of consultation, lots of patience and we've tried to say something about them being aware of the question of tino rangatiratanga, which is going to be a growing issue.

"Tino rangatiratanga is something the committee is still trying to come to grips with. I don't think it is understood around the country either. If you asked fifteen different iwi, you'd get something different from them all. I think there is a big mix-up as to whether we are talking sovereignty or rangatiratanga."

Don's own feeling is that sovereignty was something for kings and queens, which meant nothing to Maori when the Treaty was signed, so the Maori chiefs very happily told the Queen's representatives they could have sovereignty. "They said the Queen could have sovereignty over those Pakeha rabble rousers in Russell because the Maori signatories were being told they were chiefs, which they knew they were anyway. Then over the last one hundred and fifty years, successive governments have gradually gutted that rangatiratanga."

His understanding of rangatiratanga is the right of the iwi to have a say over the issues that affect them as a people. He says in one sense it is not asking for any more power than any other landowner or ratepayer. But in another sense – because the government has promised to meet the principles of the Treaty of Waitangi – it requires careful thought.

"We've got to try and come up with a formula that is going to help local governments around the country to understand the depth of feeling behind tino rangatiratanga and I don't think we are doing that very well yet. I think we are saying that we will agree to what the RMA expects us to do but we don't really want to go as far as letting Maori have a real say in all the issues that affect them. I think there will have to be some very careful discussions, some giving and taking on both sides, to fully understand it. I think also, that a lot of Maori have got to sit down and think what they mean by it too."

He says it is a new way of thinking for local bodies. When they are preparing a regional soil plan, for instance, they need to think of the spiritual value of the soil. "There is a value to land, to soil, to forest, to sea, to water that Maori instinctively feel, that a lot of us don't understand. The land is a commodity for us to use. For Maori it's part of them and something you share but don't necessarily use."

Don has a dream that one day New Zealand society generally will understand all the viewpoints on these issues. "We've probably got to do a fair amount of clearing of the eyes so that we are seeing exactly what Maori mean when they say they feel part of the land. I think a lot of Pakeha are starting to believe that. Lots of farmers who have changed land from rough scrubby gorse into highly fertile producing land, they've got an affinity with that land. But it is in a different way because they can still sell it for x number of dollars whereas not many Maori nowadays would sell land."

A concept that many local bodies are beginning to understand is that of kaitiakitanga. Don says Maori in the Opotiki district do not feel alienated from their kaitiaki role. He says about two-thirds of the area is Maori-owned land so he believes they feel like guardians of what they hold.

"Yeah. They feel in control. They don't pay rates on it!" he jokes. "Although I laugh about it, that is a growing concern. Maori see the rates as a Pakeha form of tax on something that they would not tax."

Rating is one of the more challenging issues the national consultative committee is considering. Don says there is also an Internal Affairs committee looking at the whole rating question. "There are some real issues with Maori land, particularly multiple-owned land that will never be productive. One or two councils are experimenting with defining what is productive and what isn't and whether there are degrees of that, and whether you can adjust rates to suit. But under our present rating systems in New Zealand, rates are either based on capital value or land value and both depend on productivity."

Getting Maori to participate more in the political process of local bodies is one of Don's objectives. However, he is not keen on establishing special seats or a Maori ward system to ensure that representation. He calls that tokenism and does not believe it will achieve the best results. He says Maori must be empowered to feel confident to stand for public office.

Local authorities have faced the brunt of protests over Maori sovereignty in recent years. In the neighbouring local bodies of Whakatane and Kawerau, Don is aware of the declaration of sovereignty by Tame Iti of Tuhoe. "I'm not sure that Tuhoe endorse what Tame is doing. I think until he's able to convince his kaumatua and his people that what he is doing is right, I don't know how far that will go."

At one of the fiscal envelope hui in Opotiki, Tame carried a ladder into the hall and spoke to the Minister in Charge of Treaty Negotiations, Doug Graham, from above – capturing media attention. However, Don says, displays which make the headlines or television news are not always useful in informing the public about the issues.

"I think that while the fiscal envelope was rejected quite soundly everywhere, it opened up a whole area of discussion and opportunity that will be important in years to come.

"Moutoa Gardens had the spotlight of the country on it; I think rightly so. It was a local issue that needed the input of local wisdom and understanding. I think nobody won from the events at Moutoa Gardens, but nobody lost either. The people at Moutoa Gardens were trying to assert their need to be heard about what they were wanting. Perhaps they had a feeling that they hadn't been heard and had to take some drastic actions to do it. I think probably that the council thought they were listening – but perhaps they were listening and not hearing."

He says there are a lot of lessons to learn from the Moutoa Gardens occupation and the biggest lesson is to keep an open mind. He acknowledges that many Pakeha were frightened by the incident but thinks their fear may not be justified. "Like what happened in Auckland at the Asian Development Bank conference. I think if people haven't really sat down and thought out carefully what is being said they will be frightened by the fierceness or the anger perhaps. I wonder if we are a little too frightened in New Zealand sometimes by people who stand very strongly for issues that they're concerned about, or whether we have lost our ability to do that."

Don believes New Zealand does not need to separate into Maori and Pakeha forms of government. He likens the Treaty of Waitangi to a marriage certificate and the concept of separatism to divorce. "If all you do towards your partnership is sign your certificate you won't stay together very long. But if you sign your certificate and then you work at your partnership, you stay together.

"We can use history to ensure that our future is a stronger place, not to beat each other over the heads. We should use history to ensure that we don't allow a repetition of those wrongs. That is what the Minister of Justice is trying to do and I have respect for that. I'm not sure his government fully understands what he is trying to do. I think there may be some difficulties within there. But I'm sure he has a very clear concept of where he's trying to get to."

He cannot believe there is a need for Maori to have their own nation or their own parliament and he says it is impractical, too; because the population is becoming more and more a mix of Maori and Pakeha.

"I think the idea of a separate Maori parliament is a knee-jerk reaction – an easy way out, like a divorce. If your marriage is breaking down it's not easy to sit down and talk the thing through and get it back together again. Perhaps that's one of our troubles in New Zealand. We dissolve partnerships too easily. I guess part of it also is I have a feeling that there's a spirituality within people that can get on top of the divisiveness."

Don has a clear concept of what is needed. He calls it equity. And he says by strengthening Maori, Pakeha will benefit, too. While he dismisses the idea of Maori sovereignty he is absolutely certain that rangatiratanga is an issue of great importance to New Zealand. "I'm just waiting for my Maori friends to tell me what it really means."

## SUE CULLING

*"People ask, 'Isn't Maori sovereignty just about giving power to Maori over your life?' I say, 'No. That was never what was envisaged in the Treaty.' Because my ancestors were slaves I'll never be a slave for anybody and I'll never agree to that kind of juxtaposition of power."*

Sue Culling (nee Menzies) is the National Co-ordinator for the funding agency CORSO, a community worker, trainer and educationist.

She is married with three sons, aged 21, 19 and six. Her husband, Tony, is a teacher who shares her political ideas. The couple and their eldest son are part of a group called Freedom Roadworks which operates like a large supportive family. The 14 adults – Pakeha, Maori and Pacific Islanders – are home schooling their children and "building a future on the basis of Maori being tangata whenua." They do "decolonisation work" on themselves and any other groups on request.

Sue Culling's ethnic background is British and African. She was born in Dunedin in 1950 and went to St Dominic's College for all her schooling. From 1978 to '82 she, her husband and two eldest sons moved to England, but most of her life has been spent in Dunedin.

Through CORSO she has become involved in a number of initiatives to recognise Maori sovereignty, the latest of which is the Taitua Ki

***Awhitu Trust, set up in early 1995 as a joint project between CORSO and Ngati Te Ata.***

From the age of eight, the girls at Sue Culling's school would ask her: "Who are you? What are you? Where do you come from?"

"So I always knew I didn't fit. That is the irony of living in a place like Dunedin. Of my family I am probably the darkest. I used to say to my Mum and Dad: 'What am I? Where do I come from?' Dad would always say: 'You are a Kiwi just like everyone else.'

"It was not until I was about 12 that my mother finally told me that my father's grandfather was a Spanish Negro. I didn't have a clue what that was. It could have been a pirate on the Spanish Main. It could have been anything."

Gradually, over the next 30 years, Sue Culling pieced together the story of her great-great-grandfather, Joseph, who had been a slave from West Africa, taken to Antigua in the Caribbean and then transported after emancipation in 1836 to Tasmania.

It had not been discussed openly in the Menzies family because Sue's father found it very painful. "He denied that side of him and acted snow white. He was influenced by his environment in Invercargill where he was poor, Catholic and black and you couldn't have more disadvantageous factors than that. Also, his mother was a widow, so he had no father to protect him."

In 1993, while attending a conference in Venezuela, Sue travelled to Antigua and found some relatives there. When he was transported, her great-great-grandfather left behind a common law wife and six children, so some of Joseph's descendants still live in Antigua.

"For me it was always important. Politically it has made me what I am. It has made it difficult because in this country of dual cultures – Maori and Pakeha – often I didn't know exactly where to fit. You know you're not Maori. You know that you are Pakeha, but you know that Pakeha don't really trust you, because you look like you are not really Pakeha. There are all those sorts of things that used to operate in the eighties. But I'm very comfortable in my skin now."

Sue says it has influenced her attitudes to racism. Right from a young age she knew racism made her sick. Her stomach started churning when she encountered it. "That would be the more overt kind. But in New Zealand some of it is so subtle."

It is ironic that Sue had to go to London before she really began to understand how racism operated in New Zealand. She and her husband, Tony, decided to leave because they "could not stand living under Muldoon any longer" and while they were in England they joined the London Maori Club.

At the club Sue met a Maori woman who talked about her whanau. "Her father had told her to be really careful of Pakeha. There were certain things you never told them. You never told them your right name. There were lots of protections put in place for her as a kid. So I explored this. What is it about Pakeha that other people are frightened of, and even hate?

"I was shocked to find out that things weren't as harmonious as people were led to believe. Coming from the South Island there is also this myth that all the bad Pakeha were in the North Island fighting Maori for their land, but down in the South Island it wasn't an issue for us because it was all above board."

In Sue Culling's view South Islanders need to understand the effects of colonisation on Maori as much as anyone else. She and a colleague from Freedom Roadworks run decolonisation workshops to help Pakeha and other tauiwi, such as Pacific Islanders, to find "what their vested interest is in Maori sovereignty."

"We evaluated all the work we did in the eighties and we decided that the movement hadn't achieved much. There were a lot of people who knew about the Treaty – it was being taught in law schools and so on – but the situation for Maori hadn't got any better, and Pakeha people were able to argue all the clauses and all the language but weren't prepared to do anything."

Sue and others in her group decided that they had to deal with "emotional blocks" which she believes prevent Pakeha people taking any action. "Even if they actually saw it was just, and what had to happen, then there was always that emotional block, that fear, that stopped them saying, 'Yep, we're going for that!' So that's the work we do."

Their workshops include structural analysis and an international view of colonisation. People learn why colonisation took place and how it affected everybody, not just Maori. "There were losses that Pakeha incurred as well which have to be acknowledged. That's one of the reasons they don't move because they've got too much pain of their own."

Sue claims that a crucial factor which is always denied is the pain of not belonging. Pakeha insist that they do belong but she says deep down they know they do not. "We need to grieve for that – accept that we can't go back – know that we have to stay here and work out what we are going to do. Unless we do that, we're never going to give energy to making things different and getting off Maori people's backs so Maori can go for sovereignty."

In the workshops Sue and her colleagues try to explain what forced Pakeha ancestors to leave their homes and go somewhere completely alien, knowing that they would never see their family again, and what it felt like.

"We talk about the difference between the people who initiated the process, the colonisers in England and London who saw it as an extension of the British Empire, and those who left the Highlands of Scotland, the potato famine in Ireland or similar problems in England."

The workshops also discuss the way many settlers forgot their roots; Sue claims that an integral part of successful colonisation is to forget who you are. She also tells Pakeha that many of those who came to New Zealand had no control over the colonisation process. She says it was early financiers and speculators like Russell and Whitacker who shaped the way this nation would look.

"It may make them angry about what happened to Maori but they don't feel guilty. It gives them motivation to work for something better rather than feeling so guilty they can't get past the fact that they shouldn't be here and that they caused all this trouble."

Sue's definition of Maori sovereignty is borrowed from Maori lawyer Moana Jackson. He talks about it as "the power to define and the power to protect". "And that is what Maori people had, and were sure that they could retain. And, of course, it's what has been taken away from them."

During the eighties, Sue was involved in the black women's movement and watched many splits develop. She realises now that they were necessary because she says people needed to go back to their own communities and find out who they were and then get the strength to move forward again.

"Now we talk about it as being a time of coming back together. So it's knowing what your role is and what your place is and being really strong about that, not being shy or embarrassed and not being a slave."

"One of the things that people ask is: 'Isn't Maori sovereignty just about giving power to Maori over your life?' I say: 'No. That was never what was envisaged in the Treaty.' And I don't deny that there could be Maori people who want that. But maybe because my ancestors were slaves, I'll never be a slave for anybody and I'll never agree to that kind of juxtaposition of power."

Sue says Maori sovereignty is important to her because it is a justice issue. She also has a belief that things would be better if Maori people regained the control they always exercised. "That does not mean I will support any Maori bureaucrat or capitalist who wants to just come in and privatise everything and rip off things like the Europeans taught them to do. And it is not to say that I support Maori individuals and say, 'Yes, because you are Maori you are better than everybody else.' That sort of subservience died in the eighties as far as I'm concerned. But it does mean that I have this deep faith that Maori people, as iwi, know what is needed for this country.

"Nowadays Maori are consulted about a large number of issues in New Zealand but when it actually comes to them having any control, Maori considerations are overridden by so called 'national interest', 'the good of the majority' or 'overwhelming economic interests'."

She contends that sovereignty is also about making mistakes. "So many liberal Pakeha don't believe that Maori can do it properly, do it right, so therefore they don't trust them to do it at all."

Sue says this lack of confidence is often unspoken. She gives as an example what happened in CORSO at the time when there was a big debate over whether an Aotearoa fund should be set up to assist Maori people. Many members of the organisation were not convinced that Maori were as needy as the overseas groups they traditionally worked with. The compromise was that people who wanted to give to Aotearoa could donate to a special fund if they wished. Then another, more critical, debate erupted. This time the argument was over who would administer the new fund.

"A lot of people were quite happy to fund Maori people as long as they could decide which Maori it was going to be. It could have been radical Maori or conservative Maori, but the Pakeha had to have that control."

Normally when CORSO allocates funds it has groups within its own organisation who take responsibility for certain parts of the world. Sue and some of her colleagues saw the Aotearoa fund as an opportunity to devolve the power and move away from the inequality of the donor/recipient relationship. Since then the funding agency has also been changing its relationship with recipients in other countries.

"Of course a lot of people weren't happy. I suppose CORSO being a leftie organisation, the Maori they wanted to fund were those who were politically correct – with a socialist agenda – not necessarily Maori people who wanted a Maori nation. They would say things like 'Nationalism is fascism' and 'Look what is happening in Fiji'."

The coup in Fiji had already caused a split in CORSO, which from Sue's perspective reflected similar Pakeha attitudes to indigenous people. "Whether you support the coup or not, it was still indigenous people trying to take control of their lives. If you are talking about sovereignty they are entitled to do what they can. And we all learn anyway. But there was an assumption in CORSO at the time that Fijian people didn't know how to manage their own affairs – that the people wouldn't sort it out, that in the long run it wouldn't get sorted out – because the people were too dumb to think.

"That is what operates with most white people. Whether they say they are anti-racist or non-racist or whatever, deep down there is that belief that there is the rightness of whiteness and there is only one way and it is our way, whether you are a socialist or whether you are a conservative or whatever."

CORSO's small Aotearoa fund was eventually placed in the care of a multi-tribal Maori Putea Committee which decides its own criteria and priorities, and how the putea will be allocated. At the same time CORSO agreed to fund a Maori organiser to work in his or her own tribal area for the needs of the tribe – asserting tino rangatiratanga.

Sue sees that the issue of "a Pakeha institution getting off Maori backs" is as important as the process of setting up the fund. "But just making that decision to let go of the control of those crumbs was more than some people could hack and they left CORSO."

The first Maori organiser began work in 1986 in Kaitaia, the next was based in Parihaka and the latest, Waatara Black, works from Ngati Te Ata south of the Manukau Harbour. CORSO pays the organiser's salary and expenses, and he or she has a commitment to tino rangatiratanga.

"Ngati Te Ata already exercise kaitiakitanga and rangatiratanga in the context of where they are, so Waatara Black has been able to do a lot of work in the Auckland area. She is one of the consultants for the Auckland Regional Council. The iwi have tons of paper to wade through from all the bureaucrats. Waatara has the ability to organise that stuff because she is not trying to earn a living as well."

CORSO's most recent venture to recognise Maori sovereignty has come about because of Waatara Black's role as an organiser. It is known as the Taitua project; involving 50 hectares of land on the Awhitu Peninsula. Ngati Te Ata had wanted this piece of land for many years because it was one of the few blocks of rainforest left in their rohe.

Sue says they wanted it for cultural and spiritual reasons because it was a food source and sacred site for the tribe. It features magnificent trees, a reminder of the dense forest of puriri and kauri which once covered the whole Awhitu peninsula. In 1992 it came on the market.

"We tried to buy it but the owners would not sell to CORSO because they thought we were going to 'give it to the Maoris' and they did not want 'radical Maoris' as their neighbours. Ngati Te Ata were quite devastated. They tried to get DOC to buy it. They tried to get the local council to buy it, but instead the council bought another piece of land down the road they said was better."

The land was sold privately but CORSO did not give up. They wrote to the new owners explaining why they wanted to buy it and asking if they would consider selling. At first the answer was "no" but then in 1994 the owners' lawyer wrote to say that CORSO could have first option. "They were really nice people and they kept extending the time so we could put things into place to try and get the money to buy it."

Sue says it was "really freaky" because CORSO is not good at raising money and they needed $100,000 to go ahead. She sought advice from a fund-raising consultant and had begun raising the money when she learnt that Ngati Te Ata had been approached by DOC who were prepared to buy it. Sue was disappointed.

"I thought it would kick the guts out of our project. We couldn't have it on Crown land because the land was the important thing; for Ngati Te Ata to be able to work there. And for CORSO it was a chance to explore the concept of Maori and Pakeha working together. We wanted to have it as a new model of a working relationship. And we knew no one would give money towards it if the Crown was involved. So I said, 'We'll do it. We won't let you down.'"

Afterwards Sue felt nervous about what she had promised. However, in March 1995 CORSO bought the land and by July 1995 they had raised almost $150,000, mostly in small pledges. Nearly all the donors were Pakeha. Banks declined CORSO's request for a mortgage on the land. Instead they were given a loan from a trust in Dunedin, made up of CORSO and several other groups, who borrowed the money on their own CORSO building.

Sue has found Pakeha very enthusiastic about the project because they see its potential and they want to be part of something positive. For Ngati Te Ata it provides a place to regenerate the native bush and seed stock to reafforest other parts of the Awhitu Peninsula. Members of the iwi will also work in an education centre to be built on the block. They hope to attract eco-tourists, particularly young people, who will stay there, work in the bush and learn about the natural and historical environment.

The Taitua Ki Awhitu Trust has five trustees. Two are from CORSO (of whom Sue is one) and three are from Ngati Te Ata. There is also a team to manage the bush on a day-to-day basis which includes other people in the district, Maori and Pakeha. A botanist from Auckland University, Ewen Cameron, has agreed to advise them on how to look after the forest.

The land has not been vested in the tribe yet. Sue says it will be eventually, but in the meantime it serves both groups' purposes to have a working model of something they are building together. "Because the fear for Pakeha is that they don't have a place. The only thing they see happening is the government ripping off Maori or Maori coming in with a big stick and hitting everyone on the head and saying, 'We're in control.' So it is really important to give people that kind of hope and say it really is possible. It does work. Here you are! So that they can actually let go some of the fear and move.

"I'm not saying this is the model for the future. But I'm saying we have to have some positive models so that people can get over the things that hold them back from actually supporting Maori control."

CORSO has had little real support from Pakeha environmentalists for what the Taitua Trust is doing. Sue says relations between them and Maori are strained by the conflict between the concept of a Garden of Eden and sustainable usage of forest by indigenous people that is generations old.

"Maori probably wiped out some species but they've done nothing compared with the ravishing of the world that Europeans have done. So why do Pakeha environmentalists think they are entitled to occupy the moral high ground? I don't think indigenous people anywhere in the world have treated their natural environment and resources the way Europeans have. It's all very well to look at the tiny picture, but when you look at the whole big picture, it looks quite different.

"Maori people over time did learn about preserving their environment but a lot of that knowledge has been lost because of colonisation. People expect individual Maori to know about those old conservation values but individual Maori don't know. The whole structure of learning and all the ways that Maori taught each other were largely destroyed by colonisation. That relearning needs to happen and it's not going to happen overnight."

Sue says Pakeha conservationists need to understand that the only land left to Maori was the worst land. "The economic base that Maori enjoyed and the numbers that were sustainable have been destroyed so nowadays Maori need to survive as best they can. It's all very well for environmentalists to say they have to protect the Waitutu Forest or whatever, but we live in a cash economy where you have to have an economic base to survive. That's the kind of world that Maori people have been forced to live in.

"And even the stuff that is being destroyed now is being destroyed worldwide at the behest of European companies or transnationals. The logging of rainforests is not being done because the indigenous people are doing it voluntarily. There is a whole experience of colonisation which has brought those people to where they are."

Sue believes that Maori sovereignty is important for all New Zealanders because of what has been experienced by everyone in the last 12 years. "It is almost as though we have nowhere to go and nothing left. And Maori people regaining that control, that right to protect, that right to define, will mean there is a future for us and for our kids."

She is talking about the increase of foreign investment and control in New Zealand. As an example, she cites the hundreds of applications for foreign investment processed since 1990 of which only a handful have been turned down. She says that includes a great deal of land which has been sold largely to Americans and Australians.

The answer, Sue says, is to make New Zealand uninviting for transnationals and other interests. "Supporting indigenous people is really destabilising for multi-nationals. So support for Maori people, Maori nationalism or Maori sovereignty is going to be an important factor in whether these companies want to come in and buy up the country."

Trade agreements like the GATT are also taking away control from New Zealanders in her opinion. She says other countries will dictate which pesticides are legal here and whether producers can sell irradiated food, for instance. "The health of New Zealanders is not even in our hands. Our health and well-being will be in the hands of people overseas who want to make money out of trade.

"Those things are all part of the Maori sovereignty picture. It is about all of us having a future here, about Maori controlling the things that are needed for them to protect us all. I believe Maori were given this land to look after. For me there is nothing clearer than that. It wasn't given to Pakeha. We were given lands in Europe and other places and our ancestors chose to leave them or had to leave them.

"Most people I know don't want to live under the kind of democratic system we have now and I don't believe MMP is going to change that a hell of a lot. They don't want a hierarchical government with white men sitting at the top having all the control. They don't want a country where foreign nationals and companies can come in with a lot of money and take whatever they like."

Sue doesn't have any firm ideas about what a future political structure for New Zealand should look like. She likes the idea of a participatory democracy that is devolved in communities. In 50 years she believes it may not even be necessary to have a nation state.

She acknowledges that any revolution of this sort is more likely to be seen by her children's children than during her lifetime. In fact she has been disturbed by surveys among young people which show that they are entrenched in their white culture and want it to stay supreme.

"I think that some of the things that have happened in the school system in an attempt to make people sensitive to Maori have actually been counter-productive. I don't think schools or tertiary institutions are the right places to raise consciousness and politicise Pakeha because of the emotional work that has to be done. You can't teach it in a classroom. The blocks are not intellectual. If you don't deal with that then you just get educated racists and people who are freaking out with the fear of loss."

While Sue does not think it is her place to suggest any new structures to recognise Maori sovereignty, she says two strands of Maoridom have to weave together, the urban and the tribal. She says those strands will need to work out a way for Maori people to benefit as a whole and then for everyone to be looked after.

"As every culture changes and evolves there is a lot of work to see that young people have a say and that women have a say. So my hope is that Maori will do that work and not have a structure like a House of Ariki. I hope any structure will actually reflect all Maoridom rather than just the hereditary chiefs. It's still up to them, but what I see happening leads me to hope that something other than that will evolve."

As for Pakeha, she says they should work together for Maori sovereignty in their own families and communities. "So that when change comes the people you really want with you are there and not on the other side of the barricades."

**PETER MUNZ**

*"Assimilation and colonisation are the essence of human history. You can try to stop it or slow it down but you can't prevent it no matter what you do."*

Peter Munz is Professor Emeritus of History at Victoria University in Wellington.

He was born to "a totally secularised Jewish family" in Germany in 1921. His father died when he was very young and most of his early life was spent in Italy until he and his mother and sister came to New Zealand as refugees in 1940.

Professor Munz studied history and philosophy at Canterbury University in Christchurch and after the war went to Britain to gain a PhD in medieval history from Cambridge University. He has lived here permanently since 1950.

He has published 12 books, the most recent of which are The Shapes of Time: A New Look at the Philosophy of History, Our Knowledge of the Growth of Knowledge: Popper or Wittgenstein? *and* Philosophical Darwinism: On the Origin of Knowledge by Means of Natural Selection. *He has also contributed to many academic journals and edited and translated several books.*

*Peter Munz is quick to point out that he is not an expert on New Zealand history although he is familiar with the works of colleagues who are. His opinions are based on his knowledge of medieval European history.*

*Broadly, he says, the British have done to the Maori what the Roman Empire did to the Britons 20 centuries ago and what the Normans did to the Anglo-Saxons after 1066. He says his wife complains that he always thinks in terms of thousands of years. "But that is my profession. I'm an historian and I take very long views."*

It took Peter three years to realise that New Zealand was not entirely God's own country. Stationed in Temuka for his first teaching job in 1943, he was taken aback when his landlady assured him that he would really like New Zealand once the Labour government was got rid of; and he was disgusted when she warned him not to sit downstairs in the local movie theatre "because that's where the Maoris sit and they've got fleas." It gave him an inkling about prevailing attitudes towards Maori but he had few opportunities to learn much else.

At Canterbury University New Zealand history was not discussed and it was not possible to study it. "What we did was imperial history and how the world had been made happy by British expansion." Much later, in 1960, Peter broke the ice at Victoria University when, as Acting Head of the History Department, he invited Keith Sinclair and Bob Chapman to give the first lectures on New Zealand history there.

During his studies and early years as a lecturer Peter saw an occasional brown face but he thought them no different from other New Zealanders. "I've got a fairly darkish skin, too. I'm not all that white myself." By and large he was not aware of any racial discrimination and still regards New Zealand as an extremely tolerant society.

"What has influenced me enormously is the experience of my adolescence where people were persecuted and killed for their race. So when people mention the word race I see red. It's a wrong concept and a nonsense word and ought to be eliminated from our vocabulary because it refers to nothing more than skin colour and the shapes of noses. Cultural differences are undeniable but the word 'race' has no meaning!

"You see, there are no genes for Maori or for European or for white or black. Skin colour refers to nothing more than the amount of sunshine one can tolerate."

In Professor Munz's view, assimilation and colonisation are the essence of human history and you can try to stop it or slow it down but you cannot prevent it no matter what you do. "All societies are the outcome of assimilation. England, France, Germany, America, India, China consist of amalgamated ethnic groups. They get absorbed. They assimilate themselves with each other and something new emerges. All this fuss about preserving ethnic purity strikes me as completely ridiculous. It merely serves to detract attention from real problems and genuine grievances. No ethnic group on earth is 'pure'."

Peter has been influenced by his own loose cultural ties – born in Germany, feeling most at home in Italy where he grew up, intellectually based in Oxbridge but domiciled in New Zealand. He encourages others to be as diverse in their outlook.

"Already Pakeha have ceased to be all that English and Maori will eventually cease to be all that Maori. I can't see any virtue in either preserving our Englishness or in preserving our Maoriness. We will all come together and be Kiwis all of us."

He is doubtful that Maori language can survive into the future, comparing it with other languages, once highly valued, which are no longer spoken. "Ancient Greek, Latin, Anglo-Saxon and High German were all marvellous languages but no one speaks them any more. Languages are changing and you can't keep them in a glasshouse. What is happening all over the world is that everybody will fall into English and English will change as a result. Even in Japan, all over India, Africa and America. It is absolutely inevitable.

"To learn English is not to submit to the 'dominant' culture. When you look at England today you can hardly call her dominant. To learn English is to learn the language of mankind and make yourself understood on six continents."

Peter believes it is unrealistic to be "over-protective" of cultural identities. He says while one must be absolutely tolerant of cultural difference, different cultures should all live side by side and not arrogate political power for themselves. "I can't see how because you want to be Catholic or Irish – or you want to be Maori and have a lot of maraes – why you have to have political power as a group over and above the power every individual enjoys as a citizen."

Here his medieval history comes into play. He draws parallels with the Anglo-Saxons who lived in England before the Norman conquest. "Imagine if people in England said we must preserve Anglo-Saxon culture. The Norman conquest was at first hard on them economically and politically, but gradually they emerged, and I don't think anyone in England now would get hot under the collar for not being Anglo-Saxon.

Anglo-Saxon has gone down the drain. Nobody speaks it now. Most people can't even read it. Modern English is vastly different.

"It's nothing to do with 'I am the dominant culture and the minority culture must be squashed out.' All cultures sooner or later get squashed out and assimilated to new and other cultures."

Peter Munz is rarely "politically correct" and frequently argues with his fellow historians about Maori issues. He says it is a shame that under the charters of tertiary institutions teachers are obliged to be "PC" because in his opinion it forces them to hide the truth.

One of his best friends is Bill Oliver, who wrote *The Story of New Zealand*, and he is full of praise for Jamie Bellich ("a student of mine") who has just written a "stupendous" new *Penguin History of New Zealand*.

"Bill Oliver probably suspects that I am a little bit impatient with the demands for ethnic separateness. I think he is right there.

"Many people think that nations and societies and ethnic groups' identities are permanent fixtures. But when you study the history of the last 2000 or 3000 years you realise that they come and go and there's no ethnic identity which lasts very long. That includes Maori. Some Maori think they came here ready-made in canoes. But they didn't.

"The people who came were really Polynesians and probably practised a culture that was more like the islands they came from and had the same sort of language. They came here and hunted and gathered food, and when the moa were exterminated, and when their archaic culture in the North Island gave way, they started to reorganise themselves. There was a great change without outside interference. And so there started the Maori cultures which lasted for 200 or 300 years. But it is not a permanent fixture. When the Pakeha arrived the cultures started to change again."

He has observed a huge change even in Pakeha society since he arrived here during the Second World War. "It was perfectly all right for this boarding-house woman to say to me, 'Maori have got fleas, don't mix with them.' Nowadays I don't think anybody in his or her right mind would even think a thing like that, let alone say it. In 1940 when I came here, Pakeha New Zealand was a very bigoted, uptight society. Uptight about sex, uptight about religion, uptight about everything. Fifty years later they are more relaxed and tolerant."

Peter's views about New Zealand society are more in harmony with Maori when he talks about the growing gap between rich and poor. He feels very deeply about this issue and the way that Maori figure highly among the unemployed and lower socio-economic groupings. However, at this point he diverges again.

"The Treaty of Waitangi worship and idolisation is not addressing the real problem. And I think that Maori themselves are very misguided if they think that their underprivileged status is caused by the lack of implementation of the Treaty of Waitangi. There are other reasons and I think they should be addressed and given top priority. I think that instead of all this propaganda about the Treaty of Waitangi there ought to be real input into urban Maori, improving education and parenting. None of these problems are going to be solved by the advancement of separate Maori identity and cultivation of the Maori language."

He is an admirer of Sir Tipene O'Regan whom he calls "hard-nosed" because this Maori leader is determined "to get his hands on money and resources for Maori education and to build up this underprivileged underclass."

Reading New Zealand history pains Peter, although he is not surprised by it. "The way the land was confiscated and the people were cheated out of their land was morally reprehensible. I suppose, however, it could not be stopped at the time. This terrible process had many similarities with the enclosure movement that took place in Britain during the eighteenth century. Just as Maori wanted muskets, Pakeha settlers needed land. I'm very glad now of course that this is changing and they are trying to redress these injustices."

When it comes to redressing these old injustices he sees problems which transcend moral and legal considerations. There is a clash between two incompatible economies. "The Maori economy was a subsistence economy and they treated land very much as a sacred place to be lived on. I take it that this is what tangata whenua really means. Whereas Western economic life is not a subsistence economy and land isn't a sacred thing to be on but it is a marketable commodity."

His historical background leads him again to compare other times and places. A conflict of economies also occurred in Europe "with heart-rending ferocity" at the end of the Middle Ages. "Such conflict cannot be resolved by staring at Maori and English words in the Treaty. Whatever they mean, they will be ground down by the harsh realities of the market."

Peter says land must be returned in a way that makes it more than something just to be treasured as sacred sites, so that Maori can raise capital on it, develop and exploit it. "Simply to say, 'That land is holy land for us to live on', that is in conflict with the needs of modern society and does not help, least of all, Maori."

The Middle Ages provide more parallels for him. "This is what really first attracted my attention. In early European history the ethnic tribal groups were very much like the Maori groups here in New Zealand before Pakeha arrived. They were small land-based communities, much like hapu and iwi, and they lived entirely by subsistence farming and hunting. They had exactly the same sort of attitude to their trees and they worshipped rivers and brooks and they buried their dead and worshipped the ground the dead were buried in.

"And this lasted until the arrival of the Romans, until the first and second century AD, and then it started to change rapidly because the Romans offered remuneration for slaves, furs and minerals. So the tribal people of central Europe adjusted themselves, just like the Maori did in the early nineteenth century. Very rapidly they knew which side their bread was buttered on and hoped that contact with the newcomers would raise their standard of living. But by satisfying all the Roman demands it started to destroy their own iwis and hapus. So they emerged and reformed themselves as totally new kinds of societies under warrior leaders – which remind one of Te Kooti and Te Rauparaha or Titokowaru."

Peter dismisses the 1835 Declaration of Independence as simply a gesture directed against the French who were trying to come here. ("Without it, they might now be using Banks Peninsula to test their disgusting bombs!") Similarly, he says too much is made of the Treaty of Waitangi.

"What happened was that there was a ticklish situation developing and Busby and some other people thought it would be a good idea to have a political gesture to calm everybody and draw everybody together. So they drew up this Treaty and it was drawn up in English and Maori, and the Maori version doesn't completely coincide with the English version. There were a whole lot of words that were untranslatable and nobody knows exactly what was in the mind of those who had a hand in it."

He claims that the two societies who entered into the Treaty are no longer here. Maori were in the majority in 1840 and that has been reversed. "Since the Treaty was signed Maori have changed their language, dress, religion, occupation and way of earning a living – and become enormously assimilated."

Similarly, Pakeha society is no longer just British but a mixture of many races. "If you talk about partners, who are the partners? Queen Victoria is dead, her successor looks like she is going to be abolished. The Maori chiefs who were the other partners, I understand, really no longer exist. The tribes are now run by trust boards and to claim that those trust boards are direct embodiments of the chiefs who signed the Treaty of Waitangi is stretching historical imagination to the point of fantasy.

"I think it is unrealistic to talk about Maori self-determination. If you live in an ethnic group in a geographical boundary, self-determination could certainly be viable. Here in New Zealand, Maori and Pakeha geographically are completely mixed. There certainly are areas where lots of Maori are living but you haven't got a geographic area you could set aside.

"And if you do what they did in the United States – I think this is absolutely appalling – to set certain reservations aside and lock the Red Indians in and supply them with food and beer and leave them to their own destiny. This is the most demoralising thing you can do to anybody. South African-style homelands, ghettos or any other form of apartheid is degrading and socially and morally unacceptable."

Holding such strong views it was inevitable that Professor Munz would find himself in hot debate with Maori and it was even more likely in the university environment where he was working.

His first confrontation occurred on the faculty at Victoria University in the late sixties. At that time arts students were required to study a foreign language for their degree and a Maori lecturer suggested that Maori should be added to the list.

"I objected to this on the grounds that Maori hasn't got literature like Russian or French and therefore it couldn't do the same educational job. My Maori colleague objected and said he had five thousand 'spells' on tape and that it was as good a literature as Dostoevsky's *Idot* or Moliere's plays. I could not accept that any number of 'spells' were comparable to Dante and Dostoevsky and so it became a very angry confrontation."

On two other occasions Peter has challenged aspects of Maori culture he found difficult to accept. The first one was prompted by something Sir Paul Reeves (a former pupil of Peter's) said when he was Governor General. "He said Maori elders had approached him very worried that information they had given to New Zealand historians had been put into books which were being sold in shops for money. Reeves defended and sympathised with these worries. I suppose he was really appealing to historians to stop the habit."

Peter wrote to a newspaper calling it "the beginning of the dark ages" where certain knowledge was "private to certain priests and common people were not allowed to share it."

"If that sort of thing is the essence of Maori culture, I don't like it and I don't think it is very suitable for a society that is supposed to be open and free and democratic."

He says the other incident occurred when a study group headed by a Maori woman criticised the university curricula because they made knowledge available to everybody and allowed everybody to discuss and question it. "It was even suggested that a Maori monitor ought to be stationed in every department to protect knowledge from being bandied around.

"She wrote that, to Maori, knowledge is something sacred that is only to be divulged and passed on by word of mouth to specially selected people who are entitled to it by birth. I found this absolutely unacceptable – especially in a university, but I would say unacceptable all round."

When the university decided to bestow degrees at graduation ceremonies on the marae Peter wrote to the University Council saying, "Since a university degree is awarded as a result of free and critical discussion of everything under the sun, it would be inappropriate and misleading to bestow such a degree on a marae on which women may not speak during ceremonial occasions and where protocol is guarded by sacred tradition which is not open to criticism.

"Though it would be politically correct, such a graduation ceremony would be a betrayal of the untrammelled search for knowledge. A marae, for ceremonial purposes, is what sociologists call a 'closed' society. A university is an 'open' society, the presiding minds of which are people like Socrates, Copernicus, Newton and Darwin – that is, people who were not afraid to be culturally *in*sensitive by questioning and challenging received wisdom. On a marae, by contrast, the presiding frame of mind is respect for elders and for tradition. Marae and universities do not mix easily."

He says it took centuries for Western universities to free themselves from domination by the church. Now, he contends, they are being invited, for the sake of political correctness, into the bondage of marae protocol.

The idea that Maori have some special status as tangata whenua is one that Peter rejects. "But how indigenous are they? They may be a few hundred years before Pakeha. I mean they are not natives. They came from other islands like everybody else. We are boat people all of us.

"We always think that colonisation is a unique thing that has happened in the nineteenth century and that it only happened to so called 'coloured' people. But it has happened before and empires always have the same sort of effect. They draw other people in and together. The whole of European history really began with the intrusion of the Romans into central and northern Europe. The Anglo-Saxons who came to England were not very different, by and large, from the Polynesians who came to New Zealand. There are enormous similarities."

If he has a general view of New Zealand's future it is for social justice in an open society. He has been disturbed by the effects of the economic restructuring over the past decade. "I find it absolutely unacceptable how the beneficiaries of this new development are building their town houses and running their Porsches and yachts all over the place and consuming a disproportionate share of wealth; and how a whole lot of people are becoming poorer and poorer trying to feed their children with cheap food they cannot afford; when everybody, and I mean *everybody* is making a contribution to the total wealth, which is being distributed unjustly.

"I cannot understand why people are just standing by and tolerating this and imagining that the implementation of the Treaty of Waitangi – whatever that might mean – will help. Pitting their hopes on the Treaty reminds me a bit of a Cargo-Cult!"

While he cannot accept the idea of Maori sovereignty he also rejects the political and social order which ignores the fact that there is an underprivileged class where Maori are far more numerous than Pakeha.

"In fact, the other day I admired Ranginui Walker. I don't always agree with him. But he said in a radio interview that he wouldn't be surprised if before long the underprivileged Maori would gang together with the underprivileged Pakeha and demand some kind of change. I thought it was an absolutely marvellous idea because he is suggesting that they address the real problem and forget the imagined problems of sovereignty.

"As things are, we may well be heading for confrontation. It will occur not because of race but because of underprivilege. In any society where there is a large group of underprivileged people who are not sufficiently educated, who are socially and economically disadvantaged and whose family life is such that they can't pull themselves up – you know poverty, metaphorically speaking, is a hereditary occupation which gets passed on to the next generation because of these disadvantages in your family – now that is a real problem.

"I find any social order which does not address this problem is wrong. It ought to be changed before they have a situation like the one they have in the USA. And this is where race confrontation might come in. It may look like race confrontation but, in reality, it will be class confrontation.

"Come to think of it, Mike Smith could have made better sense if he had taken his chain saw to one of the legs of the Business Round Table, instead of attacking the tree on that Auckland hill!"

### JANE KELSEY

*"Sovereignty is the most central critical issue to the future of New Zealand because Maori are mobilising with increasing militancy around it. The longer Maori sovereignty is not addressed, the stronger those demands and movements will be."*

*At 40, Dr Jane Kelsey is an associate professor of Law at Auckland University. She is a prominent Pakeha commentator on Treaty of Waitangi issues and is known as a strong advocate of Maori self-determination.*

*Jane comes from "conservative" Irish/Swiss stock on her mother's side and French and "narrow Methodist" stock on her father's side. They had settled in New Zealand for three generations but Jane was born in Sydney where her father was working for some years. Half her childhood was spent in Australia so she had minimal contact with Maori. Her mother's family farm in Taranaki was called Sentry Hill although Jane says it was a very long time before she thought about what the name meant.*

*After completing an undergraduate law degree at Victoria University she continued her study overseas at Oxford and Cambridge. Until she returned home to New Zealand in 1979, Maori remained peripheral in her awareness. She was plunged into Maori issues when she began a research project with Auckland gangs in that year, and was soon caught up in the world of Treaty politics.*

*Jane Kelsey is a strong critic of the economic and social costs of New Zealand's economic reforms over the last decade and is particularly disturbed by the impact of increased foreign control on Maori aspirations for self-determination.*

*Her book* **A Question of Honour** *was an analysis of government policies involving the Treaty of Waitangi from 1984 to 1989.* **Rolling Back the State** *(1993) and* **The New Zealand Experiment – a World Model for Structural Adjustment?** *(1995) are her two latest publications. She is in demand in many forums as a speaker on Treaty issues.*

When Jane Kelsey began teaching at Auckland University at just 23 she quickly became part of "a political movement that was moving very fast and which had a constant overlapping of people". The network included feminist, anti-nuclear, anti-racism and Maori rights groups.

"Times were very different then. While most Pakeha were ignorant about the Treaty, we were a generation bred on activism and debate. People were prepared to speak out, to protest, to ask questions and to learn. My family had always encouraged that in me. It's very different from the narrow, insecure climate we face now. Many of our generation have become complacent or withdrawn, while the 'children of the market' seem reluctant to explore alternative ideas."

She remembers how vigorous the debate was at that time, with the impetus provided by the revival of Maori language, culture and militant politics. "Most of this passed Pakeha by. They were just coming to grips with Tony Simpson's book *Te Riri Pakeha* and understanding that there was another version of colonial history. In terms of Pakeha awareness that book was important.

"At the same time Pakeha anti-racism groups like ACORD (Auckland Committee on Racism and Discrimination) were insisting we had to take responsibility for being Pakeha. That wasn't very popular at the time – like when ACORD forced an inquiry into the treatment of children, mainly Maori, in Social Welfare homes. We were trying to look not only at the issues of racism and state abuse of children – which was horrific – but also to understand the connections between the over-representation and the abuse of Maori kids in Social Welfare homes and the whole political Treaty issue."

The Springbok tour in 1981 "had a bandwagon" effect of bringing in a lot of Pakeha who might not otherwise have become involved in Maori and Treaty issues. Police confrontations during the tour and at Waitangi protests in the following two years, a new occupation at Takaparawha and then the Hikoi in 1984, brought a swathe of arrests and court cases. Jane, as a lawyer, helped with defence strategies – focusing on political issues to be raised in the trials by people defending themselves.

Under the weight of increasing pressure from Maori, supported by the anti-racism movement, the Labour government in the mid-eighties introduced the concept of "biculturalism". The system was supposed to become more "culturally sensitive" and "appropriate". Jane was sceptical about this approach because she thought it created irresolvable tensions with the Treaty.

"Biculturalism was tinkering with the system. Rather than defusing the issue, Treaty debate became more and more focused and more and more rigorous in its demands that tino rangatiratanga issues be addressed. That's still very much the tension that underpins the biculturalism policy in the public service today."

"Partnership" is another term she calls "a nice fuzzy buzz word" from the eighties which avoided dealing with the question of power – "as though partnership is possible when one party seizes power, then claims to be superior and treats the other as subordinate."

"The Treaty is about a relationship between two sets of representatives talking about how they would co-exist in the future and on what terms. I prefer to talk about co-existence and co-operation."

She is quite clear about what the Treaty of Waitangi means and that those who say it is ambiguous simply do not like what it says. To her mind "tino rangatiratanga" in the Treaty means independence – just as it did when the expression was used five years earlier in the Declaration of Independence. "Kawanatanga" was a subordinate and delegated authority.

To call the Treaty an equal partnership is nonsense to her mind. To separate out the three articles of the Treaty is also nonsense. She says it is a document imbued with tino rangatiratanga which is talking about a relationship of co-existence in the future.

"It may be that Maori are prepared to make concessions about that relationship today. If that is the case that is what needs to be established through dialogue. But it can't just be a unilateral re-interpretation of the Treaty as the Crown and the courts have attempted to do. And until those negotiations and dialogue take place the issue will remain unresolved."

Although she insists the role of Pakeha is to "sort out our side of the Treaty bargain" Jane Kelsey has put her foot in it a few times herself, as a Pakeha trying to support Maori struggles. She has failed to consult on issues and done things on the spur of the moment that "seemed the most sensible and helpful things to do without actually checking them out." At times some relationships with Maori were strained. She had to be self-critical and try again. "People judge you on your track record and if you screw up it's a matter of rebuilding."

She knows that some Pakeha find that an excuse to do nothing. They think whatever they do they will get it wrong so paralysis sets in. She calls that a cop out. "The problem is once you know something is unjust you can't unknow it. You have to work out what to do. I think also that in the early to mid-eighties we, as Pakeha, didn't really handle that very well. Pakeha anti-racism worked a lot on the negative and not a great deal on the moving forward and visioning."

Nowadays anti-racism tries to take a constructive approach by building a belief among Pakeha that there is a "win win" situation for Maori and Pakeha. Jane calls it "empowering, instead of disempowering". She tells Pakeha that the enemy isn't Maori; the enemy is "the state and foreign capital" because it leaves both peoples without any control over their lives.

"The way forward is to draw the connections between the insecurities, alienation and sense of loss of control that many Pakeha are feeling as a result of the last decade's changes – focusing in particular on foreign investment and foreign control – and the way that Maori are saying the same thing.

"Some of the most militant of Maori are saying, 'We are prepared to work out how we can co-exist, how we can make this into a dynamic forward-looking country where we actually have control collectively. You need to respect our authority and in that process we will respect your right to be here.'"

Jane believes the Maori sovereignty issue is finally being taken seriously because the focus has shifted from the good faith and obligations of the Crown onto issues of investment and economic and political control. She also believes that the government assumed it could ignore or repress Maori dissent when it took place at home, but could not cope once it was taken offshore. "When Maori moved into the international sphere the effect was enormously potent. The government's carefully nurtured image of New Zealand's success story was being damaged by people telling the truth."

Examples she gives of Maori using the international stage are the Sealord fishing rights issue which was taken to the United Nations, the strong Maori presence at the Geneva talks on the United Nations Declaration of Indigenous Peoples and the international networking by the Maori Congress and people such as Maori lawyer and activist Moana Jackson.

Likewise, she says, the government could not control international debate during the protests at the Asian Development Bank conference in Auckland in May 1995. "Maori were very strongly asserting their right to be part of any international dialogue – political or economic – and the lack of any mandate for the colonial government to speak on their behalf. They also sent a clear message to international financiers and others who were intending to take advantage of our 'open door' that they do so at very considerable risk."

About the same time the occupation of Tamaki school came to a head. Jane finds it significant that the Chinese buyers threatened to withdraw from the deal because they were upset about the behaviour of the police, and because the government had not been up-front with them about what was going on.

"Foreign investors would be wise to look at what happened in Mexico. There indigenous people, supported by sectoral groups who shared their concerns, mobilised to bring the free market economy almost to its knees. Those foreign investors who blissfully seek to take advantage of opportunities and rape economies without any sense of social responsibility can expect to reap very negative rewards."

For Jane this highlights the political significance of the Treaty in the future for Pakeha. "Who do we side with? Maori who are fighting for the same things as many Pakeha are arguing for; or the government, which is responsible for the mess, and big business from here and overseas who are cashing in? As Pakeha, we need to realise that it is Maori who are raising the issues and questions which are crucial to our future and our life in this land."

In Jane's view sovereignty is the most central critical issue to the future of New Zealand. "Maori are mobilising with increasing militancy around it. The longer Maori sovereignty is not addressed, the stronger those demands and movements will be. As we have seen in 1995 that will involve a combination of young and old, rural and urban."

The constitutional dialogue would need to recognise the role of hapu in signing the Treaty. However, she says it would be difficult to ignore what has happened to Maori society since then – disruption caused by the anti-tribalism of colonial politics, fragmentation, denial of political leadership, individualism, removal of resource bases and the huge effects of urbanisation. "These are things that Maori themselves are working through. Pakeha understanding of the Treaty relationship and our relationship with each other is being left far behind."

Jane insists it is not for Pakeha to dictate the terms of constitutional reform or it will never work. "If we genuinely want to resolve these questions then Maori have to be given the space, resources and authority to sort their position out. That's already starting to happen. Pakeha need to support the right of tangata whenua to do that. But we also have to work out where we stand. Only then can we engage in real dialogue. That can't take place through the Waitangi Tribunal or the courts, which the Crown controls. It has to involve genuine constitutional dialogue."

She shows a reluctance to discuss what institutional structures might emerge until the function of such a body has become clear and grassroots debate has taken place. "It's nonsense to start designing new institutions for 'power-sharing' until we are clear what issues they are going to address. Instant solutions like suggestions that we co-opt the Anglican Church model are absurd – especially when there's plenty of doubt about whether the model even works for the Anglican Church! We have to get the process right. That will take time, and genuine commitment on everybody's part."

She advises the government against trying to control or co-opt the process of discussion among Maori about constitutional issues. She believes the government has tried to do so in the past and has succeeded only in being a catalyst to force the debate even further.

"Maori have the right to determine those questions amongst themselves, rather than the government coming out and dictating what it will negotiate on, through what particular format, and selecting whom it will recognise and give that task to."

She also warns that Pakeha powerbrokers cannot rely on "divide and rule" the way they have in the past. "There is a real difference between the past and now. In the past those talking about the Treaty and Maori sovereignty were seen as a bunch of radicals and activists who didn't have mainstream support; as a passing phase. All the deeper things that were happening in Maori society weren't apparent to many Pakeha. Today they are deeply cemented as a political issue of central importance to where the country is going. They have to take the issues seriously."

In 1995 support for the activists has appeared from unexpected quarters. "When you've got Sir Charles Bennett coming out in support of Annette Sykes, you've got the Maori Battalion – who've always been used by the colonial state as the epitome of those who will fight for Queen and country – being seen to change sides. Of course most of them haven't changed sides. They are more likely just saying what they have said in private for years. But the changing public climate is very clear."

Some Pakeha interpret tino rangatiratanga as the exercise of authority at a district or regional level, parallel with local government. Jane Kelsey believes this is a way of avoiding the real sovereignty issues. "Maori authority needs to be recognised as equivalent to government power at the national level. Then it can be exercised as hapu authority at a local level."

She says there was an opportunity for this to happen when the Waitangi Tribunal recommended the recognition of kaitiakitanga for the Manukau Harbour. She believes a whole range of local issues such as sewage disposal and depletion of fisheries could have been addressed.

"If those hapu responsibilities and obligations were conveyed to Pakeha as constructive and positive, many would have wanted to support them. Again, I don't think local governments have attempted to explain those benefits because they see it as them losing power. That's fundamentally what the whole question is about; those who currently hold power being prepared to realise that they hold it illegitimately and that they really have no choice now but to debate how they share it. If they debate it now, it can be a constructive debate. If they don't it could get very messy indeed."

Jane is a republican but she knows that any decision to make New Zealand a republic would create another set of complex questions for Maori to resolve. What would happen to the relationship with the Queen, the mana of the Queen and the status of the Treaty? Would it open the way for a renegotiation of the Treaty?

"I have absolutely no doubt that if a process of constitutional dialogue were set in place with Maori, that had an agreed agenda, then very sensible decisions could be made. But it would be a fundamentally different world of political and economic power from what we live in today; which is why no mainstream political party is going to place those things on the table voluntarily."

In her view, the structure of Pakeha politics works against sensible debate. "The Alliance Party and New Zealand First have policies which are very strong on the foreign investment and control issues and at the same time claim to support tino rangatiratanga and Maori sovereignty. If they are prepared to draw the connection between those issues and present them publicly then we might be able to have some constructive debate on it, and force Labour out of the closet on the question so that it will have to come to grips with it. But political parties tend to think in the short term – 'What will happen at the next election where Pakeha have the majority of votes?' And the polls show that gut racism is still more powerful than rational forward-thinking debate."

New Zealand's current form of parliamentary democracy has failed to accommodate Maori aspirations. Jane says that is because it was born of empire and colony and patriarchal voting systems and is full of structured inequality and elitism. She says there would be no problems whatsoever in addressing tangata whenua and tino rangatiratanga issues in the context of a genuinely "participatory" democracy.

"If the goal of democracy is that people have some say and control over their lives then it means rethinking the systems we have; not nostalgically and defensively trying to hold on to institutions that didn't serve the interests of a great number of Pakeha people, as well as Maori."

While she will not discuss possible structures for addressing Maori sovereignty Jane Kelsey does have a list of key issues she says must be addressed in talks with Maori.

• Revenue and taxation. She says they are absolutely vital to the discussion. That includes not just income tax, corporate tax, asset tax and local rates but also things like levies on foreign exchange transactions.

• Foreign policy. What are the obligations and to whom? What international relationships are involved? How does foreign policy relate to recognition of indigenous people and indigenous nations? Peace issues are also relevant.

• International trade agreements. The responses that Maori have made to the GATT particularly in relation to intellectual property rights are an example of the issues here. Who has the mandate to negotiate such agreements?

• Resource management, environmental and conservation laws. These debates have been under way for some time.

• Health and education. What form should these services take? To what extent would iwi exercise authority?

• Defence. Debate over the purpose of defence forces and where they are to be deployed.

- Immigration. Jane sees the Treaty of Waitangi as the immigration charter that entitles Tauiwi to be here. "It is for Maori, not Pakeha, to say who is welcome in Aotearoa and on what terms."
- Economic policy and foreign investment. Jane sees this as the stumbling point because she says economic policy is the driving force of everything that happens in New Zealand.

"Authority has shifted over the last decade from the colonial government to international capital and a corporate elite. It will be exceptionally difficult to unwind most of that. That area of foreign investment and control of the economy is the crucial question that everyone faces in the country today and I am absolutely positive it will be a key focus of Maori sovereignty movements in the future."

She warns that refusing to engage in the debate will not make it go away. Even conservative Maori leaders have warned that increasing disruption and eruptions will take place until the question is addressed. "We will see unilateral exercises of tino rangatiratanga. That is already taking place. Various hapu around the country are operating their own systems of government and rejecting authority from outside.

"This can carry on in little pockets until other people start taking note and doing the same. The government can cope with minor episodes but they cannot cope with systematic action. They will ultimately be forced to negotiate those terms in very unpleasant conditions if they don't agree to do so soon."

When she has offered similar warnings in the past Jane says "I've been accused of fomenting bloody revolution. But the ones who are really stoking the fires are those who refuse to enter into genuine dialogue about constitutional change while they've got the chance."

Jane says most Pakeha people and politicians have a patronising and ignorant view of Maori politics. "There is no grasp of the sophistication and depth of analysis of what is happening among Maori; not all Maori but a significant number."

A few years ago Pakeha thought Maori sovereignty had little to do with their lives. Now, Jane says, many are beginning to realise that the issue is not going to go away; it is building. "The polls still show a large aggressively redneck or ignorant element reacting to the misinformation they are fed. But there is also a deeper understanding or desire for understanding among many Pakeha."

Many people she meets find it hard, at first, to understand the connection between tino rangatiratanga and the Treaty in their daily lives. "I've found, especially talking to Pakeha groups in the last year since the visible rise of Maori militancy again, that when you actually talk through the issues they become much less threatening and people can actually understand why the reaction is like it is."

Jane believes that Pakeha are at the crossroads. The changes of the past decade have cut so deep that there is no going back. "Even if we wanted to we can't reconstruct the welfare state and the fortress economy of the past. We have to look forward; work out what kind of country we want to live in and what our values are.

"Maori are developing their vision of what an alternative future might look like. There are many Pakeha who also believe 'there's got to be a better way'. In working out that vision we cannot avoid coming to grips with Maori sovereignty and deciding where we stand."

## DOUG GRAHAM

*"I'M HAPPY TO TALK ABOUT SELF-MANAGEMENT AND TINO RANGATIRATANGA AND WHAT IT MEANS, AND KAWANATANGA, ALL THAT SORT OF THING, UNTIL THE COWS COME HOME. BUT WE ARE NOT GOING TO WASTE TIME ON SOMETHING WHICH ISN'T GOING TO HAPPEN IN A COUNTRY LIKE NEW ZEALAND."*

**D**ouglas Graham is the Minister in Charge of Treaty of Waitangi Negotiations for the National government.

His name became prominent in Maori issues when the Sealord fisheries settlement was reached with iwi in 1992. More recently he has been the central Crown figure in the fiscal envelope proposals for settling Maori claims and the $170 million Tainui settlement.

He is a former solicitor who was elected as Member of Parliament for Remuera in 1984 and became Minister of Justice in 1990. He is married, with three adult children.

Doug Graham was born in Auckland in 1942 and educated at Auckland Grammar School and Auckland University. He cannot remember learning anything about Maori at school so his contact with Maori was limited "to what my father told me of the association of the family with Maori people, what I had read in History 1 at Auckland University and a few friendships with Maori, normally in football. That was the totality of my knowledge. Not great, was it?"

At home, Doug Graham has many Maori artefacts collected by his *great-grandfather, Robert Graham, who was a member of Parliament and Superintendent of the Auckland Province in the mid 1800s. Robert Graham could speak Maori and owned considerable land at Wairakei and Thames. "And then my father had a lot of contact and used to regale us with stories of the Maori – in a somewhat patronising way, but with a great deal of humour and good nature."*

Something "odd, incredible and moving" happened to Doug Graham one morning in December 1994. He had been up late the night before finalising the momentous agreement with Tainui to settle their long-standing land confiscation claim. There had been a big hui on the previous morning at Turangawaewae and the Crown party had gone on to Hopuhopu in the afternoon to await a vote on the issue. Finally, after some last-minute negotiations, Prime Minister Bolger and Finance Minister Birch were phoned for their approval at about 11 o'clock that night.

"We were all bloody tired by that time. Then, at midnight, we all went up to Taupiri (a sacred mountain and burial place of the Tainui people) and prayed. We went back to bed and went to sleep.

"In the morning, I got up and had a few radio interviews and set off in my rental for Auckland, all by myself, feeling quite chipper. I came flying around and over the bridge at Taupiri, and all of a sudden I just found myself sobbing as I went past the mountain. Then out on the other side it just stopped. Now I don't know what that was. I don't know why it happened. But that was a fascinating experience."

Doug Graham first began to sense a spiritual dimension to the Maori claims through his good friend Paul Temm QC in the early 1980s. Paul Temm was at that time a member of the Waitangi Tribunal, along with Graham Latimer and Judge Eddie Durie.

"I used to see Paul all the time. Once a fortnight we would have lunch – at Tony's in Lorne Street normally – and he would tell me what had been going on in the Tribunal."

The two men discussed cases such as the Manukau and Kaituna River claims. Doug observed how Paul Temm was becoming more and more involved in the Maori issues he was listening to, and enthusiastic about what he was doing.

"A great man, Paul. There's a fellow who's a Queen's Counsel, a leading silk, no fool by any imagination, not one to be carried away, totally analytical – even to the point of cynicism that you get with the law. But when he saw and read things and became convinced that certain things were there, he never looked back. And his devotion to it and his complete dedication to trying to resolve some of these matters was compelling to me."

Doug found himself sharing Paul Temm's sympathy for Te Wherowhero whose lands were confiscated, "even though he had sided with the Pakeha, tried to protect the Auckland settlements and things like that – which seemed grossly unfair."

"I suppose it was the spirituality of it and some of the things that Paul said about the experiences of Maori I found fascinating. It seemed to me that it was a matter that sooner or later was going to have to be sorted out. I never dreamt that I'd be trying to sort it out!"

Doug's first opportunity to have some influence on Maori issues came about when he was on the policy committee of the National Party, preparing manifestos for the 1987 and 1990 elections. "I was keen to make certain that there was a Maori policy that had some meat to it, rather than 'they're lovely people and we don't have to worry'. Winston [Peters] was, I think, supposed to be spokesman for Maori Affairs but nothing much came of that, so I did a lot of that myself."

National is often accused of having no real interest in the Maori vote but Doug says it was not lack of interest so much as a lack of understanding and confusion about what they should do. "It certainly wasn't a matter for the agenda of national conference or anything like that."

However, he points to some positive National initiatives in previous terms – in Maori health and the introduction of kohanga reo, for instance. "I suspect that if you look back at the record of National and Labour there were probably more innovative things done for Maori under National than Labour – mainly because, I think, the Maori MPs were always Labour and they were taken for granted and never listened to."

Doug has never studied the concepts of institutional racism or structural racism. He thinks he probably could not be bothered listening to them. In his view New Zealanders are not naturally racist. "I think people get annoyed with Ken Mair and Tame Iti and don't like them. But I don't think it's because they are Maori but because they see them as troublemakers.

"I think most New Zealanders get on very well with Maori people. I think they're very proud of them; proud of the Maori Battalion, innately proud. So it's nothing like the Australians and the Aborigines or the blacks or the Indians in America."

Doug admits it has been tough going sometimes, achieving caucus support for the government's policies on settling Maori grievances, although he says there has been fair unanimity within the Cabinet, with one or two exceptions.

"I've had some right battles with Ruth Richardson, of course. I'm not saying she was opposed to what we were trying to do. But her task was to get us out of the financial mire. And that's fair enough. Everybody's vote was slashed by the razor gang and so it was a difficult time to say I needed money."

He has found Bill Birch "a bit more amenable to discussing things, a trifle less dogmatic". Doug Graham says at times he and Jim Bolger and a few others have found themselves at odds with the majority of National MPs about how the claims should be settled. "But this is the thing to do and we've got to box on."

Doug says National promised in 1990 that they would try to resolve Maori claims and at the same time stop "pouring money into the Maori Affairs portfolio never to be seen again". So their approach was two-pronged. The money from the Maori Affairs vote was to be mainstreamed and Doug Graham was appointed in 1991 as Treaty Negotiations Minister.

Doug was pleased with the appointment. "I knew it was going to be totally fascinating and challenging – that's the best part. So we set to with a will and we suddenly realised that we really hadn't the faintest idea what we were going to do."

In September 1991 the Crown sat down to begin talks with Ngai Tahu and in early 1992 with Tainui. It was frustrating for the Maori negotiators because they had to wait while the Crown worked out what its response should be. Ngai Tahu in particular was annoyed about the delay. Doug says the government had to find a way to make sure that the claims were fair in relationship to one another. It had to develop a policy for claims on mountains and rivers, and the conservation estate.

"Then all the Fish and Game, Forest and Bird, Federated Mountain Clubs and all those sort of people, got furious and thought the government was about to hand over half of New Zealand and wanted to be involved in the negotiations. Some of them are irresponsible too, one in particular. So you'd be sitting telling them what was going on and they'd go out and publish something quite the reverse. So we had some ding dong arguments there.

"We had to stop Crown land being flogged off before we could settle the claims. That wasn't easy either. I accept that a lot of the land does have to be sold. There's nothing to stop it. In Canada, most of the settlements (with native Americans) are money and you go and buy what you want. That has simplistic appeal. To retain land which may or may not be wanted is a high cost to the taxpayer."

A protection mechanism was introduced so that Maori could show why particular properties should be held back from sale in a land bank pending a decision of the Waitangi Tribunal or negotiations with the Crown. Doug says sometimes the qualifications were a "bit tight" so they needed to be reviewed. However, he says in July 1995 about 110 Crown properties had been held back from sale – "which is better than none."

When negotiating the first two big claims with Ngai Tahu and Tainui, Doug says the issue of sovereignty was never on the table. Tino rangatiratanga was, however.

"In the Tainui Deed of Settlement tino rangatiratanga is preserved and is expressed to be. Now what that means is another matter. We are not varying the Treaty in these settlements. We are correcting a wrong done. And everybody has their own view of what these things are.

"But the Court of Appeal and the Waitangi Tribunal have discussed what tino rangatiratanga actually means – and it is certainly not seceding Whanganui from the rest of New Zealand, which is what I think Ken Mair is on about.

"Issues of control of their assets certainly have been alive and well, but that's no great problem. What they're going on about is that they have to go and get their Minister's consent to $100 cheques being signed by the Trust Board – all this sort of nonsense, paternalistic rubbish. That legislation should be repealed."

In Doug's opinion tino rangatiratanga means "the right of Maori to run their own structures and their own internal structures without interference – as far as can reasonably be done in a modern society where some constraints might be required in the national interest."

In some areas, he says, that could mean Maori have more rights than an ordinary property owner but he does not know exactly what they might be.

"I think if we were able to settle the claims, vest the assets back, give them an economic base and were a little bit more sensitive to some of the issues they raise, I think a lot of this business about sovereignty would go. It's a cause at the moment. A lot of Maori people admire somebody kicking the establishment."

The kaitiaki aspects of rangatiratanga need not frighten people, in his view. He says they are concepts of trusteeship which most people would have in common with Maori. "It is more pronounced in indigenous peoples. Tainui Waikato people say, 'The Waikato River is us. It's our tupuna and if you go and throw sewage in it, we are greatly offended.' Most people say, 'Fair enough. It is offensive.'"

Doug says there will need to be recognition of the importance of the Waikato River to Tainui. He says there could be some kind of Maori involvement with the environmental management of the river at the regional council level. He does not mean that Maori should have a power of veto.

"I don't think it would be acceptable to have them saying, 'No speedboats are going to go up the Waikato River.' It just wouldn't be tolerated. I don't think even they suggest that."

When the government announced its fiscal envelope proposals for settling Treaty claims, Maori accused the government of failing to consult with Maori first. Doug believes it was not practicable to consult with Maori. "We would still have been going in fifty years if we'd started at page one consulting with every hapu."

This highlighted a problem he believes is working against Maori interests – the lack of a single body which can speak for all Maori. "I've encouraged them to try to restructure themselves without telling them what to do or being paternalistic about it. But it has become very apparent to me that the iwi autonomy or independence is very strong – and in some areas it goes even down to the hapu."

He says when there are various hapu within some iwi who all have their own viewpoint – as there are in Taranaki for instance – it may not be possible to get a decision on anything. "That is holding them back, as much as anything, frankly."

Doug has suggested some sort of kaumatua council or assembly that has the support and respect of all Maori, although he reiterates that it is not a matter for the Crown. "Who's elected and how, where they meet and what they do, is over to them. And it will take them a hell of a long time. I hope they achieve something, but I've got serious doubts."

The Maori Congress has lost a lot of credibility in his eyes. He believes they misinterpreted their role when they negotiated for iwi over the Railcorp lands. And he claims there are only five tribes who actually pay to keep the Congress operating. "That's not our fault. That's their fault. And it's sad because, in a way, it was a better Maori structure than the New Zealand Maori Council which is a Pakeha-structured thing."

The Crown's resolve not to impose new structures on Maori is illustrated in the Maori fisheries row. Some Maori have asked the government to intervene and sort out the divisions over how the quotas should be carved up but the government has refused. "The fisheries asset is not wasting away in the meantime – it's appreciating. So if it takes them 10 years, I don't mind."

Early in 1995, paramount chief Sir Hepi Te Heuheu invited all the tribes to a hui at Turangi where they made a united stand against the government's fiscal envelope proposals. At their hui the iwi also called for constitutional talks on sovereignty issues.

Doug puts his own interpretation on that. "I think Sir Hepi saw a very real risk that Maoridom would be divided and, in effect, be picked off. He thought the best thing to do was to pull all Maori together – and the easiest thing to do was to reject everything."

The Prime Minister's response to Sir Hepi angered some Maori, but Doug supports what the Prime Minister said about the government's position on constitutional talks. "This government anyway, is not interested in talking about secession or dual sovereignty, in the sense that a Maori parliament can veto the rest. I agree with Jim Bolger. That is not going to happen.

"I'm happy to talk about self-management and tino rangatiratanga and what it means, and kawanatanga, all that sort of thing, until the cows come home. But we are not going to waste time on something which isn't going to happen in a country like New Zealand."

In a speech at a Rotary meeting in 1995 Doug Graham made his position on sovereignty very clear.

> Over the years Maori have raised a number of arguments against the assumption of sovereignty by the British Crown.
>
> It is said that the Declaration of Independence, signed by a number of chiefs in 1835, should take precedence and is still valid; that those Maori chiefs who did not sign the Treaty have never given up their sovereignty; that the signatories never gave up sovereignty anyway; that even those who did sign are no longer bound because the Crown breached its obligations in various ways; or that whatever the effect of the Treaty, Maori who still claim sovereignty are entitled to do so.
>
> None of these arguments has any validity. The simple fact is that the British Crown's assumption of sovereignty, assisted certainly in part by the Treaty, unquestionably succeeded and it has, as a matter of international law, lasted. In other words, what is, is.
>
> A revolution in New Zealand had occurred, and as Professor Brookfield in his recent valedictory lecture says: "Revolution rests upon what is done, not what is legal or necessarily moral or just."
>
> It is then, a question of fact.

In some countries such as the frozen north of Canada or remote parts of Australia the indigenous people have claimed that their sovereign rights were never extinguished. Doug says no such possibility exists for Maori. "We live in a fully integrated society. The concept of Maori having some sovereign right over non-Maori or even other Maori seems untenable."

As tangata whenua who place special value on the land, Doug believes Maori should be involved in some important national decisions, such as the question of foreign control and investment in New Zealand.

As a member of the Cabinet he obviously has no criticism himself of the government's policies on foreign control and investment. He says anyone who thinks, as Muldoon used to put it, that "we are going to become serfs in our own land", should compare the level of foreign investment here with that in other countries.

He warns that Maori protests about foreign control and investment at meetings like the Asian Development Bank and CHOGM are harmful to New Zealand. "Anybody waving flags, looking like the wrath of God, shouting and abusing people, spitting and baring buttocks, that doesn't do New Zealand's standing any good at all, anywhere, for anyone.

"They can protest as much as they like but they need to realise the damage they do to overseas investment and the rest of it. Now if that's what they're trying to do – to deter people from investing in New Zealand – well, they should say so."

At one time Doug Graham, like Jim Bolger, favoured a constitutional change to introduce a senate for New Zealand which would have a very large proportion of Maori members. His choice was a House elected by first-past-the-post and a senate elected by STV (Single Transferable Vote). He says when the public chose MMP, the senate became a dead issue.

"The best thing that could happen now is for a Maori party with credibility to start up – free from political patronage of the other big parties – to stand for the things that matter to Maori people. There are good, qualified Maori people coming through. If they got in there instead of all the old faces, then I think they would have an impact which even they don't understand."

When Jim Bolger floated his ideas of New Zealand becoming a republic it opened up debate about how the Treaty of Waitangi would figure in any new constitutional structure. Doug Graham is unenthusiastic about the prospect of a republic. He believes any decisions will be at least two elections away and he cannot see any compelling reason to change anyway. He warns that if the Treaty were to be written into a constitution it could be amended by Parliament and asks if Maori really would want the Treaty embodied in legislation. "I think you'd find half the Maori would say 'yes' and half would say 'no'. What the hell do you do then?"

There are a number of interpretations of Maori sovereignty which Doug will not "waste time" discussing. If it means a Maori state breaking away from the rest of New Zealand he is not interested. If it means a dual parliament he is not interested either. If it means the local Maori people running a province, of not only Maori but everybody else as well, he calls it nonsense. "The moment we start drifting off into different flags and different foreign policy and fifteen per cent of all tax going to a small number of Maori to spend, it's just away with the fairies and it isn't going to happen!"

Some interpretations of "self-determination" concern him also. He says under international law the term has connotations of colonialism still being in place. In the draft UN Declaration on Indigenous People it has this context, which makes it an inappropriate expression for New Zealand, he says, because this country is not a colony. "Some Maori may say they are still oppressed but they are not oppressed in the sense that others are – like French Polynesia might be claimed to be."

During the United Nations negotiations, New Zealand has used the term "self-management" rather than "self-determination". "We're not trying to be difficult, but we also recognise that things are different in every country. We're not talking about the Inuit in the Arctic Circle or the Aborigine in the outback. We are talking about Maori people who live in the same street as everybody else and play football and drink in the pub the same way. So to talk about separate development and reservations where all the local indigenous people live is absolute rubbish here."

Doug Graham believes the tangata whenua status of Maori is special. He says they were here before anybody else and therefore their customary rights and their position in society deserves particular respect. It is the government's responsibility to ensure that their language and cultural differences do not die away and that their taonga are protected. However, he does not support the idea of separate laws for Maori. He says there needs to be one law for everybody and it ought to be applied fairly.

The way Maori have suffered disproportionately from the economic restructuring since 1984 concerns Doug although he thinks it was inevitable. "We know who's on the benefits and in our jails. I know the illiteracy rate, the poor numeracy, and that a lot are Maori. How do you get over that problem? You've got to give them a base of self-esteem, somewhere that's home, re-establish the marae, get the iwi to put their hand out to them again, to bring them back in. And that's how you'll make some progress on Maori crime and Maori unemployment. That's what I'm trying to do."

He applauds the plans Tainui are making to see their young people are better educated – developments at Hopuhopu and Te Rapa and two endowment colleges at Waikato and Auckland Universities for post-graduates. "Now that's what is going to improve the situation for Maori. We've failed. We've poured money into Maoridom over the past fifty years and have nothing to show for it except a lot of people in prison and all on the bottom. That's where people like Alan Duff and others are saying, 'The welfare is killing us. Give us back a chance to get going and we'll do it.'"

If New Zealand is going to avoid racial conflict he says it is prudent, as well as just, to deal with the wrongs of the past. Another factor is that the government is being forced to right the wrongs by the courts and the Waitangi Tribunal.

"So those New Zealanders who say, 'Why bother? Can't we forget it?' – sooner or later they'll have to realise that we can no longer do that, even if we wanted to. So if you had no altruism in you at all, you really have to face up to the fact that there's compulsion about this now."

Doug has faith in Pakeha goodwill towards Maori. "I think most New Zealanders deep down know only too well that we have got some baggage from the past that needs to be tidied up. They don't want to know about it. They don't want to know the detail of who did what. They want the thing settled, they want it to be final and they want the guy who's settling it not to go mad, not to go overboard."

If he is the guy settling it, there is no chance of him "going overboard" on the question of Maori sovereignty. And he is sure that that is what the majority of New Zealanders would want – Pakeha and Maori.

"I'd be most surprised, frankly, if many Maori people were in the same camp as some of the radicals. I think most Maori people, if they got their economic base back and a bit of respect – were listened to a bit more – would be quite happy with the way things are."

## MARYAN STREET

*"Maori members of the Labour Party could put up any sensible proposal, argue it cogently, and it would be accepted by the Party. There is an absolute willingness to advance legitimate causes of Maori people."*

Maryan Street became President of the New Zealand Labour Party in 1993. She stepped down from the presidency in November 1995 to devote more time to her family and her full-time job as Director of the Centre for Labour Studies at Auckland University.

Born in New Plymouth in 1955, she is a third-generation New Zealander of Anglo-Saxon stock. She describes her parents as working class with middle-class aspirations. Her father earned a moderate income in the Post Office for 41 years and Maryan says money was scarce during her upbringing. Both parents had "liberal attitudes" towards Maori.

Her schooling "reflected the colonial arrogance of the dominant culture" – repetitive units on Maori culture and pre-European lifestyle to the point where the pupils complained saying, 'Are we going to do the Maoris again!' – but no historical information about the area in which they lived, such as the Taranaki confiscations.

*At New Plymouth Girls' High School, Maryan made casual friends with some of the Maori pupils who boarded at a Maori girls' hostel. However, she says she had no real contact with Maori culture or issues until she became involved in feminism in the late seventies.*

*Maryan graduated with a BA (Hons) in English at Victoria University in 1976 and went on to become a secondary school teacher. She became involved in trade union affairs through the PPTA, moving on to hold executive positions on the Auckland District Council of Trade Unions and the Combined State Unions in Auckland. She joined the Auckland University staff in 1990 and gained her Masters degree in 1993.*

In 1981 Maryan Street would go out for regular dinner engagements with Donna Awatere, Ripeka Evans, Zeta Anich and Jane Kelsey. It was a group of very intelligent, highly motivated feminists with a strong pro-Maori, anti-racist agenda. Maryan says she was usually running to keep up.

"We would start off at one person's house for drinks and then we'd sashay off to some exorbitantly priced restaurant or other. Our favourite was Wheelers in Ponsonby Road. And we used to engage in huge debates and arguments about tactics – sometimes about principles, but most frequently about tactics – in advancing Maori sovereignty."

Maryan was acutely conscious of the contradictions of talking about Maori sovereignty in a flash Pakeha restaurant. "It was quite extraordinary. I would get caught in a wave of the white guilt that was around in the eighties, because I hadn't processed the issues enough. Thank goodness we've moved past that, because it's the most paralysing, ludicrous, unproductive place to be – caught in a white guilt trap. But at that stage I had absorbed all the arguments about gender oppression, and overlaid that with racial oppression, and I would be caught at the end of the evening thinking I should offer to pay."

When Maryan finally found the courage to say she would pay, Donna Awatere was adamant that she should not. The other women did not seem to find the dinner bills a problem, while she worried if her teacher's salary could stretch to pay her share. Just the same, she was not going to let that stop her education.

The arguments of Maori sovereignty first presented themselves to Maryan when she helped to establish a group called Feminist Teachers in 1979. She was in her second year of teaching at Westlake Girls' High School.

"It was the connection between feminism and Maori sovereignty that became so apparent. Suddenly I had some analysis of oppression, and the parallels were easy to draw. People like Hilda Halkyard-Harawira were members of Feminist Teachers. She was my age and fiercely radical. She really set us honkies back on our heels and it was great."

Feminist Teachers encouraged consciousness-raising and assertiveness training for its members. Maryan took assertiveness training with Zeta Anich and soon they became close friends. Zeta, in turn, was a friend of Donna Awatere – they had trained as educational psychologists together. While protesting against the Springbok tour Maryan had seen Donna and Ripeka Evans speaking and was impressed by them. Through Zeta she became part of their circle.

Her dinner companions have gone in different directions since then. Maryan joined the trade union movement, then chose party political processes as her vehicle and joined the Labour Party. Maryan says Jane Kelsey is still a good friend but she has not seen Ripeka or Donna for many years. She says Jane Kelsey, as a commentator on Treaty issues, is critical of the Labour government from 1984 to 1990.

"She is correctly critical of us in government in that period for the effects of our economic restructuring on Maori people. I acknowledge that absolutely. But I don't believe there was the kind of conscious conspiracy about 'rolling back the state' that Jane talks about in her book of that name. The social consequences may have been foreseen but they were not planned outcomes. There was no plan to strip Maori of sovereignty, or access to sovereignty, as she implies in her writing."

Maryan, on the other hand, does not agree with Donna Awatere's choice of vehicle (Donna has become a candidate for ACT). "However, I don't believe that Donna's aspirations have changed, although her method of realising them is different."

Recalling her childhood and her early years at school and university, Maryan regrets that she did not learn more about Maori issues. She lived only eight kilometres from Waitara but she knew nothing of the struggles of Te Atiawa, and down the coast was Parihaka which had no significance to her until she had left New Plymouth.

There were little things in her family life she remembers. Her father often used Maori words like taihoa. Her mother kept a Maori dictionary on the shelf from the days when she had trained as a laboratory technician. On Saturdays her father often went fishing early in the morning, sometimes with Maori friends. When he took the family for a "mystery drive" along the coast he would tell Maori stories about places along the way that he had learnt from his fishermen friends.

Maori stories did not figure in Maryan's studies at Victoria University until she was in her post-graduate year. "It was appalling that in the whole of my English degree we didn't do any New Zealand literature except Katherine Mansfield." She was delighted when in her fourth year she was able to study James K. Baxter.

"That was the beginning for me of meshing tikanga Maori with Pakeha values. He had a real impact on me. I met him once, just before he died in 1972, when he came to speak at New Plymouth Girls. I couldn't tell when he was reciting his poetry and when he was talking to us. I really enjoyed him. I spent a lot of time getting his poems out of the Turnbull Library. It was my first conscious thought that here was someone moving between the cultures effectively."

The last 15 years have brought many changes in New Zealand that Maryan applauds. She says there has been not only a Maori renaissance in all sorts of ways – in art, culture, political direction and assertiveness – but she believes mainstream Pakeha culture has come on board with it.

"I've always believed that you need people on the extreme ends to pull the centre over a bit. And that's exactly what has happened in the last 10 years. There is a greater understanding, albeit imperfect, of tikanga Maori, a greater understanding and acceptance of the importance of the Treaty and a greater understanding of the legitimacy of Maori grievances over land."

She says one of the most significant things the Labour government did during this time was to backdate claims to the Waitangi Tribunal to 1840. She says it did for New Zealand what the Mabo judgement later did for Australia.

"Now we argue about the process and whether it is adequate, fast enough or well enough resourced. But there was a process for addressing legitimate and long-standing grievances which you would never have got out of a National government."

In the Labour Party, she believes there is a hugely receptive and responsive attitude towards Maori issues such as representation and grievances. "Maori members of the Labour Party could put up any sensible proposal, argue it cogently, and it would be accepted by the party. There is an absolute willingness to advance legitimate causes of Maori people."

The Labour Party's structures are still monocultural and its ways of doing things are still monocultural, in her view. However, she says they have worked on that in recent years and have instituted guaranteed Maori representation at the very top of the party. There are two Senior Vice Presidents, one of which is a Maori position. As it happens, both Senior Vice Presidents at present have Maori origins.

"That went through just like that! Not a problem. Not even any argument. The ground was there and it was fertile and ready. We need to do more than we've done. There is more that we could and should do.

"In a way, what we need is a set of demands from Maori. And I'm sure they'd be met. If the demands are in the area of power-sharing then I believe they'll be met. Now that is what I understand about sovereignty. I don't understand it to be power *over*. I understand it to be power-sharing – with Maori having power over resources for things Maori."

If that demand is going to surface, Maryan says there is a need for more Maori to be "thoroughly active" in the Labour Party. There are already, of course, a large number of Maori supporters but not so many who become involved in the party organisation. Maryan says that when Maori look at how they might best achieve their aspirations, and where the most pressing needs are, they often choose to put their energy in places other than the mainstream political parties.

"If they believe that the Labour Party can help them achieve their aspirations, and they can see some success in that happening, I think greater numbers may shift what is historical support into future activism. And I would welcome that."

When Maori members put up a motion at the Auckland regional conference in May 1995 that the Labour Party should establish nationwide hui to discuss the issue of sovereignty, it was passed easily. No one spoke against the motion. Maryan says it is testament to the goodwill and commitment in the party. She says the party leader, Helen Clark, has also announced that Labour is willing to debate Maori sovereignty at any time.

"The thing that bugs me is the 'no speaks' position of the government. You know, Doug Graham on Moutoa Gardens. 'I'm not going to talk to you unless you promise not to talk about sovereignty.' Well, what the hell does he think they were there for? Does he think it was really just about this little hectare of land on this pointy bit of Whanganui?"

She found it extremely contradictory when Prime Minister Jim Bolger said he wanted to debate republicanism and then refused to have talks on sovereignty. In her book the two are synonymous. "I mean, he's nuts if he can't see the parallels."

So far Labour has not formed a policy on the republican issue, although Maryan suspects that there would be a majority in favour.

Maryan smiled when an Australian reporter rang her for comment on the debate there over republicanism. She told the reporter that if New Zealand went down that path it would be necessary to assure Maori that this would not denigrate the Treaty of Waitangi. The Australian reporter said: "But surely you just have to change the word 'Crown' to 'government'?"

"I said, 'It sounds easy when you say it quickly, doesn't it?' That is the sort of debate that is needed. There would have to be an absolute assurance that there was no demeaning of the partnership. It would probably provoke one of the best constitutional arguments we've ever had. It's a discussion the country needs to engage in. When we start to write it down, then the constitutional debate will really happen. It's going to take years.

"If we are going to truly represent the Treaty of Waitangi in our society we have to come to grips with the kind of constitutional pluralism that sovereignty implies. And that doesn't mean domination of the majority by a minority. But it means power-sharing. Now what does that mean? Does it mean there will be a separate law for Maori? Are we talking about a separate parliament? I don't believe so. I don't believe that's the issue."

What it means, she says, is institutional recognition of the right of Maori to have the Treaty of Waitangi honoured. "And by honoured I mean the right to have lands and resources returned to them where they have been wrongfully confiscated."

When Maryan is asked if power-sharing will frighten off Pakeha voters, she says Labour ought to be leading the debate about it and she claims it has begun to do that. The party has been discussing a Maori policy framework which looks at the right of Maori to manage Maori affairs.

"The Labour Party must take the majority of the population with it. So it is not a matter of saying extreme things, about how we will unreservedly give back any land that the Crown has ever had a foot in. In fact, Maori people don't want any extreme promises. What they want, as I read it, is a genuine dialogue, because the issues are extremely complex. It is about the future direction of this country. It is about how we honour our indigenous people and what being indigenous to New Zealand entitles someone to. We have to sit down in a calm, intelligent and informed way and say, 'OK, let's talk about sovereignty.'"

Maryan believes Maori would achieve power-sharing through greater representation in Parliament. She says some of the best challenges to

Pakeha are coming through the new MMP system because Maori are discussing how they can maximise their political advantage. There is talk of a separate Maori political party. "I'm not scared of that. They would be a natural coalition partner for Labour, quite frankly." However, she thinks a Maori party unlikely, at this stage, because of the diversity of Maori opinion.

It will be a long process finding clarity of thinking about Maori sovereignty, in her view. One avenue being discussed is for the Waitangi Tribunal's decisions to be made binding. Maryan believes that in the end the decisions have to be political ones although she still thinks the Tribunal has a role to play.

Critics have accused the last Labour government of cynicism in diverting Maori energy into the Waitangi Tribunal process. Maryan agrees that there were some people in Cabinet "who had no awareness of Maori issues". She is referring in particular to Roger Douglas. "I don't know what Donna Awatere has managed to teach Roger Douglas in recent times but she would have had to take him on a steep learning curve I would say. He had no comprehension about Maori issues or the social impact of his policies."

Looking back on those policies, Maryan believes there were changes that needed to be made, because without the economic restructuring the country would have gone bankrupt. On the other hand she calls the social impact "hideous".

"The effects of some of our policies, between 1984 and 1987 in particular, were devastating – for Maori working in rail, in forestry, they were ghastly. Whole communities thrown onto unemployment benefits! That social impact was the cause of much dissension in the Labour Party. The party was torn apart.

"My position has always been that we did it too fast and that we should have provided support for people who were hurt by those changes. Even today, even in an academic way, Roger doesn't understand the downside of his policies."

She says the Labour Party has shifted a great deal since then, back to social democratic principles. "There are things we can't undo, assets that we can't buy back and won't. There are some assets that should have been sold and were. But there are others that the government should have retained, in my view. We did a lot of good things. In the end what people remember is the painful bits – especially Maori. There is no doubt they suffered disproportionately."

Labour Party policies now are based on the idea that the government does need to be active in the economy, "in order to set conditions that benefit people in a way that doesn't exaggerate the disparities that are already there between rich and poor".

Maryan says it is part of sovereignty to allocate resources to Maori for them to use in the best way to meet Maori needs. "Now that resource may be disproportionate to the size of the population because the needs are greater. If that's the way it has to be, that is the way it has to be. We've always said resources need to be allocated disproportionately in order to achieve equal opportunity. That's true in Maori health and educational attainment. If Maori were freer to develop programmes that suited them, we might see more equitable outcomes."

Maryan would not like to see a government simply hand over a bucket of money and say, "Do what you like with it." She says they should be looking for something more pro-active than that in addressing Maori needs, and some monitoring of the delivery of Maori services to be sure it is working. "We need to have a way of accounting for what are essentially nationwide resources."

A major concern among many Maori in recent years is the issue of increased foreign ownership and control. Maryan calls it a real hot potato. She says it is dancing between legitimate calls for Maori sovereignty, nationhood and national identity on the one hand and xenophobia on the other.

"Overseas investment in land is particularly problematic." She acknowledges that Maori have a special affinity to the land which is not the same for most Pakeha. To her mind, foreign investment should be permitted if it works for the benefit of the country and if it respects Maori people's deep spiritual connection with the land. While 'nationhood' is a concept she can respond to positively, Maryan says 'nationalism' has a jingoistic feel to it that "scares the hell" out of her.

"A sense of nationhood, a sense of identity, that incorporates the idea of Maori/Pakeha partnership, plus a recognition of the variety of other cultures in this country, is something I would go to bat for any old time."

As she steps down from the presidency of the Labour Party, Maryan promises that Maori sovereignty will remain a priority for her as a "foot soldier" in the organisation. "It is the single most significant issue of our times and has vast social, cultural, constitutional, political, economic and legal implications. And none of the sovereignty issues are beyond the wit of Maori and non-Maori to resolve."

In her own academic field of industrial democracy she has concluded that employers and workers cannot have meaningful dialogue unless both sides have all the information about the industry before them. She says the same thing applies to talks between Maori and Pakeha – if some things are excluded from the agenda, it will not result in efficient decisions, it will create resentment and unrest.

"There needs to be a very open agenda and there need to be leaders of goodwill from both Maori and Pakeha engaged in these conversations.

"People are not going to allow our country to degenerate into violence or a kind of separatism that in the end is fundamentally very damaging. I don't think that Maori people want that. It is not in anyone's interests if we tear ourselves apart. I think there is greater interest in working co-operatively together, as long as the agenda is open-ended. They've got to be real talks. It's got to be real dialogue."

**BRUCE HUCKER**

*"The absence of revolutionary action in New Zealand is a tribute to Maori patience and flexibility which we are going to have to depend on if we are going to have a joint future."*

Auckland City Councillor Dr Bruce Hucker believes local bodies will become a major focus for Maori sovereignty issues to be tested in future. He calls himself a "social democrat with green instincts tinged with conservatism" who has considerable sympathy for Maori demands for self-determination.

Of Scottish, Welsh and English ancestry, he was born in Auckland in 1944. The family lived in the Auckland outer suburb of Otahuhu, where his father was a freezing worker. Later Bruce was a freezing worker himself during the university holidays.

He was educated at Otahuhu Primary School, Otara Intermediate and Otahuhu College, so he says he had ample opportunities to work and play and study with Maori in his youth.

Bruce gained a Masters degree in History from Auckland University and then went on to study in Dunedin to become a minister of the Presbyterian Church, receiving a Bachelor of Divinity from Otago University and an honours diploma in Theology from Knox Theological Hall. Later he travelled to the United States to study for a *doctorate in Social Ethics at Princeton Theological Seminary.*

*Bruce Hucker says his church background gave him a strong conviction about the importance of human beings and a strong opposition to injustice and discrimination. He has held positions such as Convenor of the Presbyterian Church's Race Relations Committee and Chairman of the Auckland City Committee on Unemployment. He is an active member of the New Labour Party and the Alliance Coalition.*

*He currently represents the Alliance as a councillor for Auckland City and is a senior lecturer in the Planning Department at Auckland University.*

Unemployment is a focus for Bruce Hucker's concern about Maori and their future. His first priority in dealing with Maori grievances would be to put more resources into Maori social and economic development and he says that means costs, particularly for the Pakeha middle-class.

"The film *Once Were Warriors* has implications for all of us. It illustrates the emergence in New Zealand of an underclass, some of which is Maori, in which unemployment goes through generations and patterns of behaviour become part of the culture of the group. It is going to be more and more difficult to change."

So if Pakeha are not moved by the arguments based on compensation for past grievances he offers them other arguments based on ordinary human considerations. "Unemployment leaves long-term scars. The unemployed are given a clear message. Their contribution is neither needed nor valued. The young are forced to defer their hopes and are faced with an uncertain and insecure future. Poverty and bad housing are reinforced. A sense of alienation is deepened."

If Pakeha want to protect their own self-interest, Bruce believes they should be prepared to pay the costs of tackling Maori unemployment. "The conditions are now in place that will do damage to us and to the future of our children. High unemployment rates among Maori have profound implications for ethnic relations."

Looking back on his childhood, Bruce doesn't believe he was ever racially prejudiced. There was the time he lent his straw hat, "with a nice red band on it", to a boy at school. Although the hat was returned promptly, Bruce's mother was fussy about who the boy was who had been wearing it. Was he Maori? "No," said Bruce. "His name is Hapita and he's not Maori."

Another event that sticks out in his memory was the 1960 invitation for an All Black team to visit South Africa minus any Maori players. Bruce sympathised strongly with the "No Maori No Tour" slogan even though he was only 15.

Race relations assumed an important focus as his working life in the church unfolded. He was in regular contact with Maori people in the Auckland inner city as a student for the ministry at St James Presbyterian Church and he worked with African Americans while studying at Princeton. Every weekend he travelled to New York to work as a minister in a Black church.

Back in Auckland's inner city at the age of 30, Bruce was appointed as Convenor of the Presbyterian Church's Race Relations Committee. "I was young at the time but I was appointed because of my interests and experience. In that group we developed a way of working together to ensure consensus and to make sure everyone participated in the decisions. Over time a body of knowledge and also trust grew up between people of different ethnic backgrounds, including Maori and Pacific Islanders."

Working with the Hinota Maori or Maori Synod of the church provided role models like kaumatua Hori (George) Tait, John Rangihau, Milly Te Kaawa, and Purewa and Te Ao Biddle. "These people deepened my commitment to Maori issues as well as broader human issues." More recently, as many kaumatua and kuia in the church have died, he believes the Maori Synod has become weak and too conservative, just when the wider church is turning to them for more advice and support.

In the 1970s the Race Relations Committee spoke up on some tough questions such as the Maori occupation of Bastion Point and Bruce says it was ahead of its time among the churches. However, the committee's statements were often unpopular in the wider Presbyterian Church. He remembers an angry reaction to his comments about negotiations that were taking place between Prime Minister Rob Muldoon and Ngati Whatua elders.

"We were simply asking for more time for settlements to take place after much longer discussion so the weight of the government was not too heavy on the people. It doesn't sound very radical at all but the reaction in the church was quite strong." One congregation complained that he was making it difficult to raise money for their church budget.

Bruce marched in protest against the Springbok tour in 1981 and has taken to the streets for other causes like unemployment. He has not felt the need to make a stand through civil disobedience and risk arrest. "It would depend on how serious the issue was. If it was serious enough I would. In the past I have tried to use my skills to argue and write to give support, to attempt to exert political influence."

Columns for *Metro* magazine and other articles by Bruce Hucker over the past 10 years have attempted to educate Pakeha on issues like the impact of Maori unemployment, the effects of colonisation on Maori and the collective responsibility he believes that all Pakeha must shoulder because of that past.

He summarises New Zealand history thus: The Crown made promises under the Treaty of Waitangi which were systematically and callously broken. Large amounts of land were confiscated without justification. Laws were passed which created grave injustices. The effects of breaches of the Treaty have come down to the present because a landed people were reduced to a landless urban working class. There is a connection between the way in which the social and economic base of Maori communities was shattered through the failure to observe the Treaty and the negative Maori statistics today for unemployment, educational achievement and opportunities, health and housing.

"That past has to be dealt with. If it's ignored, discontent and anger and a sense of grievance will continue to be just below the surface and boil over at different times. The absence of revolutionary action in New Zealand is a tribute to Maori patience and flexibility which we are going to have to depend on if we are going to have a joint future. The three things that Pakeha have to take into account are firstly to recognise the injustices of the past, secondly to make amends for that past and thirdly to do so in ways that create a firmer base for a joint future between Maori and Pakeha."

Despite his strong opinions about the need to eliminate Maori unemployment, Bruce has more tentative views on structures and institutions to deliver spending on Maori social and economic development. He favours the establishment of rohe pooti or regional Maori assemblies as possible vehicles. He points to current gaps in representation; many alienated young Maori, living mostly in cities, do not feel part of the authority system of the traditional Maori leadership.

"The resources have to be made available in ways which encourage Maori communities to ensure that they are spread fairly among their people. It probably means that new structures as well as the old will be needed. In the case of the Tainui settlement it was not just the kaumatua who made the decision. There was actually a vote taken. That was an attempt to consult with all of the people and to recognise the contribution of those who may not have been a part of the negotiating groups."

If there is going to be a degree of separation between Maori and Pakeha political structures he thinks it should be a prelude to coming together rather than an end in itself. This is based on his view of the Treaty of Waitangi and the relationship between Articles One and Two. He contends that it is clear in the Maori version of the Treaty that kawanatanga was ceded by the signatories. So he says there was some awareness in Maori communities that they were at least accepting the protection of an outside authority that would impose some limits on the activities between tribes. "At the same time tino rangatiratanga expressed a view of unqualified chieftainship over their taonga and the broad interpretation that has.

"I think that the links between Articles One and Two of the Treaty point to a partnership between kawanatanga and tino rangatiratanga rather than complete sovereignty being ceded in kawanatanga and simply the unqualified possession of lands, forests and fisheries that was in the English translation. That means that when talking about institutions we have to talk about institutions that are not simply carving out separate areas but are engaged, negotiating and in partnership."

A parallel Maori parliament would get Bruce's support if he could be sure that any institutions set up also involved negotiation with one another. In his view there is a clash in the idea of two peoples/one nation. "How can that equal partnership be institutionalised while at the same time retaining some form of democratic polity? A one-person one-vote democratic polity is incompatible with a view that simply deals with the status of two people as collective groups. That's one of the important conceptual issues we have to think through and it's not clear how that can be achieved."

Bruce has watched the Alliance coalition try to marry differing opinions on the Treaty question. He says the Democrats as a group are the most difficult to link with Treaty issues. Then on the other side of the coin is Mana Motuhake which is very much a Maori nationalist party.

The Alliance accepts the basic principle that the Treaty is a foundation document of the nation. "The Alliance does have an advantage that within its structures there are equal Maori partners in a system where Maori people are not in a numerical majority – which is in some ways a picture of the nation too. Certainly the Alliance will adopt policies that focus on more rapid reduction of unemployment through a variety of different measures that indirectly will have an important effect on Maori/Pakeha relations."

He sees the different strands of the Alliance coming to terms with issues still to be faced by the wider community. "In a sense it is a precursor of MMP because a lot has to be done through the forming of relationships, through negotiation and by concession rather than simply adopting approaches which say, 'Have I got the numbers? Here's a minority. Stiff bickies.' If you do that long enough the relationships can no longer continue."

The party's policy on overseas investment is of interest to many Maori. The Alliance would restrict purchases of rural land to New Zealand citizens or residents only, or to companies with more than 50 per cent New Zealand ownership. Bruce says after the alienation of large tracts of Maori land, all New Zealanders are worried about another wave of alienation to foreign interests.

The Alliance has adopted, as policy, a proposal from Matiu Rata of Mana Motuhake for establishing new Maori institutions at a regional and national level, funded by government. There would be 10 elected regional assemblies (called rohe pooti) which would in turn elect two members to a central assembly or congress. The congress would work with the government to further the interests of the Maori people, act as a constitutional guardian of the Treaty and veto any actions in breach of the Treaty.

Bruce is aware that the rohe pooti policy is not popular with Maori because it is not related to tribal areas, but he believes it has merit. He thinks it addresses the issues of introducing democracy into Maori institutions and including urban Maori. He says the policy states its support for tribal and traditional organisations as well, recognising that they will continue to play a significant role in the future well-being of Maori people.

The Alliance promises that if it were the government it would be guided by recommendations of the Waitangi Tribunal for any negotiated settlements between the Crown and claimants. It would also be prepared to negotiate for the return of publicly owned lands presently in the conservation estate or owned by local authorities, regional councils or SOEs.

The sanctity of private title would be preserved but where private land was under claim and there was consent from the landowner, the Crown would bear the cost of such settlements.

Bruce Hucker warns that in remedying injustices from the past every attempt must be made not to create new injustices. He says redress is the responsibility of all New Zealanders and should not fall unfairly on the shoulders of individuals. If privately owned resources or land are to be returned to Maori then the owners must be compensated fairly. Publicly owned land should be dealt with first and only when those issues have been settled should claims on private land be considered.

Bruce acknowledges advances that the National and Labour Parties have made in remedying Maori grievances. He points to the role of the Waitangi Tribunal established by Labour and attempts by National to negotiate claims with iwi which he says represent a significant cultural shift.

He looks back to the changes that have occurred since the 1970s. "A lot of things thought radical and strange then are now acceptable. But we still have to make advances more quickly because we are losing the race against the clock. And that's the irony. Once you have alienation setting in and going on from generation to generation the solutions that are proposed become both more radical and more separatist."

Bruce says demands by Maori to make decisions about their own destiny can also be viewed in a positive way – as a further development of the Maori renaissance. "We are seeing an approach which involves an increase in Maori confidence, increased Maori skills in a wide range of areas – even while Maori unemployment is high." He believes there is a life and vitality in Maori communities which will no longer be constrained by Pakeha systems.

As an Auckland City councillor he is most familiar with decision-making at local body level and is critical of its record in representing Maori interests. Auckland City has had few Maori councillors. There are none in the current term and the Alliance's Sandra Lee was the only Maori in the last term.

This is where Bruce has concrete ideas of delivering sovereignty to Maori. He would like to see Maori seats on local and regional bodies in the same way that there are Maori seats in Parliament. Such seats would be geographically based, just as the parliamentary electorates are, with their own Maori electoral rolls.

In Auckland, for instance, this would guarantee Maori representation on local councils, the Auckland Regional Council and the Auckland Regional Services Trust. This might mean that five of the Auckland City Council's 25 members would be Maori. Membership of the regional body could be increased from its present 13 to accommodate new Maori wards.

"In Auckland there are not only tangata whenua, mana whenua, there are a host of Maori people from other areas. It's important that the priority of the tangata whenua is respected and we might have to find other ways of institutionalising that. A seat by right for tangata whenua is a possibility."

The idea of Maori wards is not new. The Auckland Regional Authority had Maori members until they were cut out by the reform of regional government a few years ago. Since the reforms Bruce Hucker contends that things have been worse in terms of Maori political representation, especially in Auckland City. "Although there are signs of improvement with consultation and co-operation with Ngati Whatua, for instance in administering of parks and reserves at Orakei, the improvements are not good enough and are not related to sharing of political power."

Bruce says in Auckland City there have been struggles getting references to Treaty of Waitangi issues into the annual plan and the basic values of the city. Opponents claimed that if you did it for one group you had to do it for groups like the Scandinavians and the Irish as well. He calls that redneckery.

The Resource Management Act has placed new legal obligations on local bodies to consult with tangata whenua and other Maori communities. Bruce Hucker says Auckland City is taking them up, albeit slowly. "I've argued that at the administrative level there should be a Maori secretariat created which would be adequately resourced and would have a role in making sure that there was Maori input across the board in different departments. So when decisions were made Maori interests would not be overlooked as they often are."

He detects a strong reluctance at local body level to share power. He says many local bodies refuse even to acknowledge that they are part of the government. They think of government as central government. However, he says the Treaty has obligations for all levels of government as representatives of the Crown.

"One area where power has been shared to some extent at an administrative and policy implementation level is the arrangements that have emerged for Manukau Harbour and the involvement of Huakina [a Tainui environmental watchdog group] and others in kaitiakitanga roles. The next challenge for local government reform is to achieve more significant power sharing with Maori communities at the level of political representation and policy formulation."

Bruce draws the line at the suggestion that tangata whenua might have the power to veto decisions where they see their guardianship role as paramount. He says some issues involve huge expenditure and complex decisions, such as the debate in Auckland about how sewage and waste water should be disposed of. Based on traditional values, Maori prefer land-based schemes rather than disposal into waterways or harbours. However, Bruce says new values are needed to reflect increased population levels and modern relationships between people, the land and the environment.

"One issue that emerges in an industrial society is where our sewage is polluted from industrial sources with heavy metals and toxic materials. If you develop land-based schemes which involve those, you have the chance not only of poisoning the land but affecting the food chain and there's leachate into the waters. In Melbourne, a large land-based scheme is beginning to go awry and create major environmental problems which nobody wants. So what I am saying is that the more far-reaching the issues and the more potential for adverse effects, the more fear there would be of giving a veto to Maori. The right of veto gives significant power and it might be better to test it out in more limited areas of responsibility."

From a Maori standpoint Bruce believes that pressures need to be applied at local body levels if change is to take place. The occupation at Moutoa Gardens highlighted this. He regards Tame Iti's declaration of tino rangatiratanga in Tuhoe's tribal area as another sign that local bodies need to learn how to share power. However, in the end, Bruce thinks that such issues are a matter for central government rather than for local individuals.

"I work out of a theological tradition of Christian realism. And one of the assumptions of that tradition is that justice is achieved most readily through an alteration in the balance of power. In other words, unless the balance is altered justice is unlikely to be achieved because when people have power they wish to hold on to it."

Bruce Hucker sympathises with young Maori activists who are pushing for Maori sovereignty. "The issues they're dealing with show how slowly Pakeha New Zealand has come to terms with the past. They are a symbol of the way we are losing the race against time."

**STEVEN YOUNG**

*"A VAGUE DOCUMENT LIKE THE TREATY OF WAITANGI CAN SAY WHATEVER ONE WISHES TO MAKE OF IT. WHAT MATTERS IS THE WEIGHT OF NUMBERS AND RELATIVE STRENGTH AND WHO HAS ACCESS TO THE ORGANS OF POWER. NO DOUBT IF MAORIS WERE NINETY PER CENT OF THE POPULATION, THE TREATY WOULD BE INTERPRETED IN A WAY WHICH WAS VERY FAVOURABLE TO MAORI."*

Steven Young was born in China in 1948 and came to New Zealand three years later, but his links to this country had already been established. His grandfather came to New Zealand from China in the early 1900s and his father also migrated to New Zealand, with his brother and cousin, in the 1920s.

"It was the custom in those days for the Chinese to work in New Zealand and go back periodically to China with their savings to buy a house or some land; or in the case of younger people to get an education, get married or have children."

Steven was raised during the fifties and sixties in Levin where his whole family worked on a market garden, on land leased from local Maori. "I was more or less condemned to help out after school." However, because his parents were so "pro-education", if he and his brother were good at their school work they were allowed time off to study. "This involved considerable sacrifice by my parents because two *strong boys would have been very useful in the market garden in those days."*

*Steven and his brother were expected to go to university, and they did. Steven studied civil engineering at Canterbury University. His brother, now married to a Pakeha, is the Professor of Finance at the Chinese University of Hong Kong.*

*In 1978 Steven established his own practice in Wellington as a consulting engineer. He is married and has three children who are all pursuing academic careers – one daughter is studying medicine, another law and his son is in the advanced stream at Wellington College. He jokes at how stereotypical his family must sound.*

At the beginning of this century, Steven Young's grandfather worked in a communal market garden in Lower Hutt and later made a living selling vegetables from baskets carried on a pole in the classic Chinese fashion. By the time Steven's father arrived in New Zealand, they had graduated to selling vegetables from a horse and cart.

In the early 1950s the family moved to Levin to what Steven describes as a fairly typical New Zealand rural setting. "We lived near a pa – although the pa wasn't much in those days – and we had Maori neighbours and landlords.

"There were two related families next door – one with two children and the father drove a big De Soto, and the other with about fifteen children ranging in age from one to eighteen. The latter family were everywhere and got into trouble all the time."

Steven went to Horowhenua College where he became an avid reader of *Time* magazine and *Punch*. "A Chinese market gardener's son enjoying *Punch!*" He read about Kennedy, Krushchev and Golda Meir and was fascinated by stories about the American Supreme Court. He could name all the justices – who were changing the course of American society by interpreting the American constitution – and knew whether they were liberals or conservatives or interpreted the constitution as "strict constructionists".

"The Maori children were not very good at their studies, with one or two exceptions. Many of the Maori children were neglected and, in general, didn't get it together. Most didn't seem inspired to strive for anything much and dropped out at fifteen. I guess they are still in Levin or have drifted to Wellington."

At Canterbury University from 1967 to '72 Steven was a student in the "heady days of the Beatles, anti-Vietnam War demonstrations, peace, the whole human rights, feminism, sexual revolution thing."

"Sadly, because of my conservative background, I was but a bystander!"

He continued to subscribe to *Time*. "Later, I realised that *Time* is a very conservative, right-wing type of publication; but, nevertheless, the consistency of the message is very impressive." Nowadays he is a complete magazine junkie, reading magazines all week. As soon as he had the income to support this habit he began subscribing to the *Bulletin*, *Far East Economic Review*, *NBR* and *Byte*. He is also a fan of CNN. It is therefore not surprising that Steven sees the world as being based on economics or the allocation and use of resources.

"Racism is a means for one group to deny resources to another. Race and physical characteristics and religion are a convenient way to distinguish one group from one's own and to deny them access to resources, on the basis that they are different and do not share common ideals and goals. The fight against racism is a fight against this discrimination. But it must be recognised that the fight is really for economic rights and access to resources."

He strongly believes in equal rights but he says this conflicts with the fight for control and use of the world's resources – and economics is inextricably bound up with politics and power. "In order to be a ruler and to have power, it is necessary to allocate more resources to one's supporters. Since resources at all times are limited, this denies resources to another group. Put simply, in a democracy the allocation of resources is roughly proportional to the ratio of the contending groups."

"Of course, if one group is deprived of resources too much, they will start to rebel and create social unrest. They 'have nothing to lose' and will start to disrupt society."

Based on "these simple facts", Steven sees only one solution: "To move quickly to a position of equilibrium instead of wasting time on artifices such as tribal rights, Maori sovereignty and indeed to contrived readings of the Treaty of Waitangi."

Steven believes this "small country in the middle of nowhere" cannot afford to be too engrossed in its own internal squabbles or it will be left behind economically and socially. "The great economies of the world are great partly because of population, and therefore market size, but also because they have mostly relegated racial and cultural differences to a secondary role in their society."

He says the sooner Maori people have equal rights to access New Zealand's resources the better, because he believes it is a waste of time and energy to delay the inevitable at the cost of great social disruption. "However, Maori must immediately learn to take a realistic view of the world as a whole; as a large functioning, ongoing economic and political system which will not stop for a few. Not for 3.5 million people – and certainly not for 350,000 people."

In his view, Maori sovereignty has a range of meaning. At one end he sees it as a desire for Maori to administer their support services themselves. In the middle he sees it as a desire to gain control of a proportionate share of the economy. And at the other extreme he believes it is a desire for Maori to create their own country – "virtually a partitioning of New Zealand".

He is dismissive of the more arcane debates over the Treaty of Waitangi. He interprets the Treaty as having granted certain rights, and extended certain guarantees, to Maori who in turn ceded the right of government to the Crown. "Some smart lawyers now want to say that what was given to the Crown was something else – less than sovereignty.

"A vague document like the Treaty can say whatever one wishes to make of it. What matters is the weight of numbers and relative strength and who has access to the organs of power. No doubt if Maori comprised ninety per cent of the population, the Treaty would be interpreted in a way which was very favourable to the Maori. It is a valid means for Maori to adjust the social balance of power, but it should be recognised as a framework and not holy writ with immutable meaning."

Looking at his own Chinese background, Steven describes it as tribal. He says most Chinese, anywhere in the world, know where their ancestral village is located. Usually their grandfather or father would have been born there and they would still have uncles and cousins living in the village.

"In my case the village is called Ping Dee or Flat Land. About eighty per cent of the people in this village have the surname Young, while twenty per cent have the surname Leong. Traditionally, the villagers grew rice and vegetables in the surrounding fields. They are walking distance from the next village. The men practice exogamy – the men find brides from outside their own village because marrying someone of the same surname is considered a form of incest. In the olden days there would be feuds between neighbouring villages – arising from real or imagined slights – and large villages would bully small villages."

When he went back to Ping Dee he found it still wretchedly primitive. The villagers have electricity and television but no sanitation or road access.

"In my village the names of my ancestors are recorded as far back as twenty-three generations. I know my whakapapa. The Youngs and the Leongs from that village, even in New Zealand, regard each other as clan brothers, and respect and help each other and generally stick together – just like the clan brothers from other villages."

However, Steven says his clan links are becoming less and less important. His own children do not have any idea who their clan brothers and sisters might be. "I will explain it all to them one day and I will take them back to see their ancestral village. But I don't expect that it will ever have much significance to them and that is how it should be."

He regards tribalism as an idea whose time has passed. "What started out as a way for primitive groups to organise mutual help, defend territory, keep social order, care for the young and very old and transmit knowledge and beliefs is no longer required in the modern world.

"At the best, tribalism has been a useful device – a constituency for a cause – where there are historic wrongs, like land confiscations, to be redressed. There have been large-scale tribal governments in our time – Somalia, Nigeria/Biafra, Rwanda and perhaps Bosnia."

He says if Maori sovereignty means some form of government based on race it is a retrograde step and doomed to failure. "Such a proposal would be divisive, socially disruptive. We will end up with another Bosnia – with the equivalent of Bosnian Serbs fighting for a slice of New Zealand about the size of the Wairarapa.

"At one level I support the preservation of Maori taonga and culture because they are unique and indigenous to New Zealand. Where else can they be preserved? At another level I am bound to say these treasures are meagre compared with the cultural treasures of the rest of the world and its civilisations. I count among these the written languages and literature, science and technology – and the concepts of democracy, human rights and law."

He finds it ironic that Maori activists are flying to hui, communicating by cell phones and faxes, taking out High Court injunctions against the sale of radio frequencies and signing contracts leasing fishing quotas. "Yes, of course they must use every means to press their case for their rights and treasures, but do they reflect on the great treasures of the rest of the world they have acquired and use as a matter of course?

"New Zealand has something to learn from Maori culture. Some family relationship and group dynamics, and respect for the environment and sustainable use of resources. But the Maori have a great deal to learn from the rest of the world too."

He says most societies have moved away from tribalism towards a melding of peoples – a meritocracy – which offers wealth and power to those who can exploit information and knowledge. "We cannot be stuck in a world of argumentative iwi and hapu looking for new ways to share a small cake.

"I despair when I hear of one tribe, with a sparsely populated territory, advocating distribution of fishing quota according to coastline length, while another, large, tribe takes out an injunction to stop this and advocates the distribution according to population. What has this got to do with the Treaty of Waitangi? It has everything to do with the allocation of resources – and greed!"

One of the issues which has brought Chinese and Maori people into debate is immigration. Steven assumes that, under Maori sovereignty, Maori would have a greater say in immigration and it would not be in Maori interests to have more non-Maori coming to New Zealand – even, he says, if it is in the long-term best interests of the country.

"If New Zealand wants foreign investment it will need to accept some degree of immigration. If it asserts that it is part of the Asia Pacific region then it will get Asians and Pacific Islanders. As the Indians said in England, 'We're here because you were there!'

"It seems so difficult for some Maoris to see their place in the world as opposed to their place in New Zealand. Both are important. But if you are the richest man in the poorest country you are still poor."

He believes that Chinese immigrants bring a new perspective on achievement, work and enterprise. They also show that things can be done another way – with fewer resources, lean organisations and family connections.

"It must, or should, shake the Maoris to see the academic achievements of the immigrants. It would be very stupid to pooh pooh this and downgrade it as just egg-head stuff and rote learning. It is not. Education is an internationally recognised asset. To say Maoris can only achieve on their own terms is self-inflicted genocide."

When Maori and other groups protested at the Asian Development Bank conference in Auckland in May 1995, Steven saw it as naive and misdirected. He says the international banking system exists and needs to exist. Naturally the financiers would be interested in the economic stability of New Zealand and how efficiently its economy is working. However, he says, making a noise outside such a conference would make no difference to their analysis or to the level of overseas investment in New Zealand.

Foreign investment should be controlled, in Steven's opinion, but not too much. "We've got something others want. If they had it, they would make us pay. We should make them pay, too." He warns New Zealanders against being "taken in by the smart guys". However, in principle, he says, foreign investment is fine.

"In the end, this is our country – it's difficult to move land and capital assets offshore if things get tough. But we need to be consistent. Maybe we need wider consultation before some over-trained Treasury staff decide everything by themselves."

He can see some real concerns for Maori in foreign investments but he says most of the arguments he hears are xenophobic rather than informed economic debate. Steven claims that in a global economy foreign investment is inevitable, despite what the Alliance Party's Jim Anderton says. "The Maoris will not find salvation in owning their own carving factory and operating whale sight-seeing boats.

"It is important for everyone that Maori see their economic interests as similar to the rest of New Zealand. There is no such thing as Maori economics, just as there is no such thing as Maori science. The world is interconnected, inextricably interlinked."

Steven can see Maori regaining control of many natural resources – which, he says, are theirs by right. And then after that, he says they will need to make their own international contacts, sell their own trees, control their own destiny. "But they need to learn the hard lessons first. Let's not have half-baked, half-trained, self-taught, self-styled Maori entrepreneurs trying to sell prefab houses in Hawaii, earning a fat fee for themselves and then have the deal sink. Such Maori are their own people's worst enemy.

"The knowledge will come with training and experience. Training means serving the same apprenticeship as the rest of us. Formal training, on the job experience, good mentors."

Steven does not have much contact with Maori in his day-to-day life, and in Wellington, he admits, the Chinese have done little to establish links with Maori. Nancy Goddard, who has a long association with Ngati Poneke, is an exception. ("She is a Chinese woman who has made it a personal mission over forty years to help and understand their problems.")

Steven tried once to make business contacts with a Wellington Maori group but he says he found them "too preoccupied with tribal concerns to be interested in commercial reality". He says the outcome after many meetings was "politically correct" but commercially unrealistic.

Summarising his opinions, Steven says "an insidious creeping agenda towards Maori sovereignty" is going to sap the energies of this country and just waste time. "It won't fly. To encourage barristers at $1000 an hour to argue in front of the Privy Council about Maori sovereignty is nuts!"

"Simple numbers is what will change the face of society in New Zealand. The more Maoris there are, the more rights they will gain. But this does not mean economic well-being. The market will still reward the quick, the smart, the alert, the well-informed and the perceptive."

If the sovereignty argument is – and he believes it is – a device to re-allocate resources more equitably, then he calls it a blunt instrument with a lot of waste and unpredictable outcomes. "It's the long way round to achieve the obvious. There will be blood and tears and fat cats on both sides. It's really about fair sharing and access to resources, to be determined by votes. Let's accept it and get on with it. And please let's not conspire to lead another couple of generations of Maoris up a blind alley in history!"

**CHARMAINE POUNTNEY**  **TANYA CUMBERLAND**

"OUR SUPPORT FOR SOVEREIGNTY IS ABOUT LEARNING TO BE TENANTS AND GOOD NEIGHBOURS WITHIN NGATI TE ATA'S ROHE. THAT'S OUR COMMITMENT."

*Charmaine Pountney (53) and Tanya Cumberland (49) describe themselves as two middle-aged, middle-class, Pakeha women of English origins who are on a journey in support of Maori sovereignty.*

*Both were born in Auckland and attended Epsom Girls' Grammar. Both graduated from Auckland University. Tanya followed in her father's footsteps and majored in Geography for her BA and Charmaine did a masters degree in English followed by a year at Secondary Teachers College, Auckland.*

*Tanya pursued a career in Social Welfare. She held positions such as Director of the social workers' training centre, Taranaki House, and Assistant Regional Director for Development for the Social Welfare Department in Auckland.*

*Charmaine was Deputy Principal of Rutherford High School in West Auckland, Principal of Auckland Girls' Grammar and Principal of Hamilton Teachers College and later Principal and Dean of the School of Education at the University of Waikato. She was seen as an innovator in education, particularly in areas which tackled discrimination.*

*For the past three years the two women have been living on an 11-hectare rural block on the Awhitu Peninsula in the rohe of Ngati Te Ata where they are trying to work for social change at a practical level.*

Tanya Cumberland and Charmaine Pountney were not prepared to settle in a rural area until they had sounded out the local iwi. They wanted to know what the tangata whenua thought about Pakeha moving onto the land and to discuss their joint hopes and aspirations.

They had an advantage when they began to look in the Waiuku area because they knew a prominent member of the iwi there, Nganeko Minhinnick. They also knew that Ngati Te Ata had a tribal policy document with a consultative procedure to cover this very eventuality. Tanya describes it as a "sovereignty document". "In it are very clear statements of how Ngati Te Ata see the land and what they expect of Pakeha. So we had clear guidelines to work on."

It was only when the two women came to buy land that the sovereignty issue really came up for them. Prior to that their support for Maori sovereignty had involved working in anti-racism groups to educate Pakeha and fundraise for Maori projects.

"When we wanted to buy land we thought, 'Hang on a minute. That means we would be wanting to buy Maori land!'"

Tanya and Charmaine talked to Ngati Te Ata about their plans but they did not make a formal approach to the iwi until they were almost committed to buying a property on the Awhitu Peninsula. They arranged to meet members of the tribe and seek their approval.

Charmaine says it was the first time Ngati Te Ata had been consulted in this way. "We said, 'We acknowledge this is your land. We would like to come and live here. Here are our hopes and aspirations. Can we come?'"

She says the responses varied from "If you are really serious about this, can we tell you which land to buy?" to "What are you asking us for?"

The two women told Ngati Te Ata that, when they died, the land would come back to the tribe, and one of the elders asked a significant question: "What do your families think about this?"

"This question highlighted the difference between our individualistic approach and the whanau perspective of the elders."

Tanya explained that she and Charmaine did not have children so they did not feel it was necessary to advise their Pakeha families about their desire to leave the land to Ngati Te Ata. She also believed that their families would have some difficulty in understanding this decision.

"However," says Charmaine, "the tribe's perspective was that we should discuss it with our families. We still underestimate the profound cultural differences between Maori and Pakeha."

The outcome of the meeting proved satisfactory to all. Ngati Te Ata said "yes" and they were happy with what the two women planned for the land. Tanya and Charmaine believe in growing crops organically and wanted to replant native vegetation. They promised to plan any timber blocks carefully to avoid pa sites or sacred areas and not to damage the environment. The tohunga decided it was not necessary to inspect the site first because they had confidence in the Pakeha women to return anything they unearthed to the iwi.

It was a special experience for Tanya and Charmaine when, after they moved in, three of the elders came up and blessed the land.

The area where they have settled was once covered in dense rain forest; kauri forest on the east of the peninsula and puriri on the west. Only a dozen remnant blocks of native bush remain but Ngati Te Ata has been replanting native trees for years. In partnership with CORSO, the iwi recently bought a large remnant bush block which will be protected and used as a genetic seed store for further replanting. There are also plans to develop it as an environmental education and eco-tourism centre.

On the Pountney/Cumberland property the women decided to return a third of the area to native forest. They logged 150 old pine trees and used the money from the timber to fence off all the southerly slopes. Several thousand native trees have been planted and are flourishing.

"And it's amazing," says Tanya, "to see the large number of natives which have regenerated of their own accord. The seeds were in the soil or have germinated from the local bush. It shows how easy it is to restore land to its natural vegetation if you make the effort to fence it off."

Ngati Te Ata are kept informed about what is happening on the block. When the women hire equipment or expertise they check to see if anyone in the iwi wants to use it too. Cars and trailers are lent. If there is paid work to be done, it is offered first to Ngati Te Ata young people and those same young people also mind the property when they are away.

There is also an exchange of food resources. One of the Ngati Te Ata women, Waatara Black, takes them fishing or brings them fresh fish. Each season she gives them tapapa (young kumara plants) and she has shown them the traditional way to plant.

Tanya and Charmaine have researched the peninsula to see what they can find out about the history of the area. An archaeologist from the Auckland Regional Council, Ian Lawlor, has been helpful. There are signs of early Maori occupation and middens on the Pountney/Cumberland block but no pa sites.

Charmaine: "Everywhere we go we are aware of the history, so the landscape has a depth and a richness to it which it doesn't have if you think people have been here for only a hundred years. It makes all the difference to feeling grounded. You actually know where you belong if you know the history."

Most of the Awhitu Peninsula is owned by Pakeha. Charmaine explains that Ngati Te Ata moved to the Waikato during the wars because they did not want to make war on the neighbours they had welcomed there. They came back to find the whole middle section of the peninsula confiscated.

"Then there is the issue of the mining of Maioro iron sands, where there are sacred burial grounds, and the guardianship of Manukau Harbour, because Ngati Te Ata were kaitiaki of the harbour for many hundreds of years. They've been ignored as the harbour has been turned into a cesspool, against their continuing protest.

"Their experience of total alienation and exclusion is as dramatic as that of any tribe in the country, on every level – the desecration of burial grounds, the pollution of water, alienation of land. Whatever can be done to them has been done to them. Yet they also have this strong spirit and strong sense of their own nationhood. And I mean nationhood as an iwi.

"They have their international connections through the United Nations. They have their tribal policy statement. They know where they stand and what they want for the future. And they are also prepared to accommodate Pakeha within that future, as tenants and good neighbours. So our support for sovereignty is about learning to be tenants and good neighbours within Ngati Te Ata's rohe. That's our commitment."

Tanya laughs as she says that everywhere they go they talk about Ngati Te Ata and sovereignty – whether people like it or not. They challenge local Pakeha organisations and institutions such as councils, clubs and schools "to understand and work to remove their structural racism in order to develop more just and inclusive ways of operating."

The pair say that many locals know little about Maori issues. Charmaine claims that when they talked to the local Rotary Club about the Maori history of the area most of those present knew nothing about it or even the name of the local tribe.

"Some community leaders reject the knowledge. Instead of accepting it and moving forward they are always on the lookout for ways to discredit Ngati Te Ata; to fight them off, to exclude them. So we've had some interesting discussions with such people."

The pair invite Ngati Te Ata to any special social occasions on their block. When they had an open day, to celebrate being on the land for two years, two elders turned up at 10 o'clock in the morning and stayed all day talking to all the guests.

Charmaine says it was one of the first occasions that some of their neighbours had sat down and talked to Ngati Te Ata people, even though they had been on the peninsula all their lives. "It's one of the few places where Pakeha and Maori actually meet."

Tanya says they are able to mediate sometimes between the iwi and Pakeha institutions – Income Support, Accident Compensation and schools for instance.

"If Nganeko Minhinnick gets a petty letter from some Pakeha organisation she sometimes faxes it up to us, as if to say, 'These are your people.' And we accept that role. It is our job to educate Pakeha. We belong to a group to support Ngati Te Ata in their sovereignty and self-determination."

Supporting sovereignty means anything from making muffins, to finding out information and helping with submissions, or talking to local groups about Treaty issues.

Charmaine: "Ngati Te Ata cannot afford the time and energy to do basic Pakeha education on the Treaty – anyway, they didn't sign the Treaty. They're interested in the Declaration of Independence and their own self-determination. So we can do a lot of that background work with other Pakeha and that's an important role."

She believes that their neighbours and others they have met on the peninsula have a grudging respect for them. "They mightn't approve of us. They are often scared of us because we are articulate, and women on the land, and lesbians, and feminists and supporters of Maori sovereignty. They don't know which is the most frightening really! But when they realise that we are quite normal and make reasonable muffins and things, it's not so bad."

Their role can be highly practical at times. Ngati Te Ata holds an annual gala celebration on Waitangi Day to mark the achievements of their tribe; particularly children's achievements in sport, school, art or any other field. The gala is a day of speeches and presentations, music, stalls and races.

Tanya and Charmaine are always asked to run a "healthy food" stall.

On the surface it may appear to be remote from the issue of sovereignty but their knowledge of cooking has proved a resource for the iwi. Nganeko Minhinnick's son, Tahuna, an enthusiastic battler for improved Maori health, has called on them for assistance. He initiated the "smoke-free marae" movement to get his people on a healthy eating, healthy living regime and has even built a gymnasium.

"He used to ring us and say, 'Will you do some health food for a function I'm putting on, so they don't just eat the same old stuff?'" The two women prepared recipes like Mexican beans, dhal and salads. Their catering was so popular that they were asked to run cooking lessons for Ngati Te Ata women so that they could include vegetarian dishes in their catering.

As a professional woman and an educator, Charmaine says she has had to learn how to provide information without setting herself up as an expert and holding on to the power.

"One of the things about supporting sovereignty is actually being willing to share knowledge and skills on demand; not to force knowledge onto people but to make it available when it is asked for. For me the hardest thing to learn is not to try and make people do what I know is good for them – which of course is the essence of colonisation, making people do what you think is good for them!"

Charmaine first became interested in issues of racism in 1978 when as Principal of Auckland Girls' Grammar she attended a one-week course for principals on Maori education. "I began to learn a bit of what it felt like from a Maori perspective to be in the education system – the total alienness of the system – because we talked about the curriculum and what was there for Maori kids and the acknowledgement of language.

"I also began to realise that things like carvings were not just pretty decorations on meeting houses. Something about Maori philosophy and history and the depth of the culture began to sink in at last."

Tanya had reached a similar realisation 10 years earlier. As a young graduate in 1967 she went to do six months' social work in the Whanganui Social Security Department and landed up helping with enquiries in Ratana Pa. Reeling from culture shock, Tanya asked Maori Affairs for help and was sent to a small marae at Ruatoki for a Maori language immersion course.

"I was in this amazing community with about twenty or so Maori and a few Pakeha church ministers. John Rangihau was a major leader there.

So as a young naive Pakeha I had this stunning experience of living with a Maori community for 10 days and speaking no English. It was really dramatic."

Tanya's experience deepened when she moved to Hamilton to work in Maori Affairs and was taken to a wide range of hui around the Waikato. "I went through that stage of feeling totally inadequate as a Pakeha, feeling I had no culture and was nothing compared to all the Maori I was with. I had a real identity crisis about who I was and what I was going to do with myself." Those feelings of inadequacy have changed over the years to a clear sense now that, as a Pakeha, she has something to contribute and that there are ways in which Maori and Pakeha can work together.

In the late sixties Tanya worked in child welfare institutions for delinquent girls, which often put her in the position of mediating between the Pakeha staff and the Maori girls. In 1971 and '72 she trained as a social worker at Victoria University and joined the Social Welfare Department. In Hastings she found herself working again with Maori girls and their families.

A significant year for her understanding of Maori issues was 1982. Tanya took 12 months' leave without pay and during that time she accompanied some young Maori to Social Welfare. "I actually stood in the queue and it was mind boggling! For the first time I experienced what it was like to be on the other side of the Social Welfare counter. I saw them go and get rebuffed and saw how when I went up with them they got a totally different deal. That set me thinking critically about Social Welfare."

Another incident also set her mind racing. She was at a women's health gathering and heard Titewhai Harawira challenge Pakeha to stop the killing of Maori women in the health system. "I realised I had to do something so I booked into an anti-racism workshop run by Mitzi Nairn. She was a powerful influence on a lot of Pakeha. Slowly it dawned on me how structural racism works."

Tanya soon had an opportunity to use her new analysis when she rejoined the Social Welfare Department as an Assistant Regional Director (Development) in the Auckland office. She and a group of other women in the department set up an anti-racism committee and researched the extent of racism in their institution. Their report did not find favour with the hierarchy in the department and was released to the media only when someone was tired of waiting for a response and leaked it to the *New Zealand Herald*.

"A huge kerfuffle opened up. I had to deal with staff anger because the report was totally misunderstood. Social Welfare was the first government department to acknowledge the issue and use the term 'racism'. It was too strong for them. John Rangihau was asked to write another report which basically said the same things and called for change. Some superficial changes took place but really nothing changed.

"I look back now and think that I was pretty naive about how institutions work and the extent of resistance in institutions to change. I also realise that the whole concept of state dependency, of welfare, was in itself about maintaining a structure of inequality. The very existence of the department was questionable."

Tanya says Maori sovereignty was not an issue at the time. It was called biculturalism then, but, she says, it was actually about sovereignty. She has given up the idea of changing institutions in favour of helping people to identify and meet their own needs in other ways.

While Tanya was coming to terms with the concept of structural racism in Social Welfare, Charmaine was reaching similar conclusions when she heard speakers at a women's convention discuss the structural nature of oppression as it related to sexism as well as racism.

"I actually made the connections," says Charmaine. "I began to realise that oppression was not about people being nice to each other – or not nice to each other. It was actually about the way the structures and institutions worked. And so it was a real turning point for me. I went away absolutely reeling and having to do a great deal more reading and thinking."

Charmaine asked herself what they were doing about it at Auckland Girls' Grammar where she was Principal. The answer she decided was clear – nothing. Yet almost half of the girls in the school (44 per cent) had a Maori or Pacific Island background. (Maori made up about 12 per cent of the roll and increased later to 18 per cent.) She arranged for some seminars on Maori issues for staff and senior students to start talking about the politics of race within the school.

Some of the senior girls were able for the first time to really tell the staff about their experience. "I remember a beautifully groomed prefect who was Samoan saying, 'I have sat in the school for four years now and there are some teachers who cannot tell any of the Polynesian girls apart in the class. And there are some teachers who have never learnt to pronounce any of our names.'"

Maori students at the school also began to challenge Charmaine and the staff about what they were doing for Maori students and what they were doing to acknowledge Maori in the school. Sharon Hawke was one. She brought her political awareness from the occupation at Takaparawha. Another pupil, Katarina Pipi, after she left school, brought a film for the staff to watch called *Race Against Time*.

"In the film, these adults were talking about what happened to them at school and what an alienating, hostile experience it had been. It was the views of a wide group, from street kids to university graduates. It wasn't just people the staff could write off. It was people they had to listen to."

Charmaine was excited by the challenges rather than feeling guilty. "I felt stupid because every time I learnt something I thought, 'Why the hell didn't I learn that sooner?' But I knew that I was open to learning and certainly wasn't defensive or anxious about it. The young Maori and Pacific Island women in the school, and their mothers, were so supportive and so loving and kind about it all that it wasn't too difficult inside the school. What was happening outside was much harder. I had some real struggles with the board."

She remembers feeling shame once about the funding of a new Maori Studies room for the school. For two years Maori students had been raising money to pay for carvings and weavings until one day a new guidance counsellor at the school, Linda Smith, who is Maori, asked Charmaine why Maori girls had to raise money for what was an essential teaching base in the school. "She said, 'You don't ask the phys ed kids to raise money for the gym equipment or the art kids to raise money for art equipment.'

"I said, 'Oooh, no. We don't, do we!' This was the mid-eighties by then and we were still making those assumptions – that anything Maori, Maori people had to do or pay for, that we had no obligation somehow. From then on, when anything was suggested for Maori students I demanded that it be paid for directly from school funding, the same as it would for any other students."

In 1985, when Charmaine returned from a Nuffield award in England, she went to the Vice Chancellor at Auckland University with a plan to look at structural racism and sexism in the university. She was a member of the university council at the time. All that the university would agree to do was to circulate a questionnaire. It asked what the various departments were doing to include Maori people and culture, and women and women's knowledge within their programmes.

"The answers were so revealing about our leading academics at the university! Only two departments responded openly and with positive statements to the survey – Continuing Education and History. All the others replied with varying degrees of violence and vituperation. 'What ridiculous questions are these? There is only one kind of knowledge and this is academic knowledge, international academia.'

"All this utter nonsense which has been completely discredited around the world! What can we expect from this country when that was the norm among our leading academics?"

She, too, has chosen to work outside institutions in fighting racism. She has the freedom to opt out of the system because she began drawing on her superannuation on turning 50. Charmaine also does freelance work as an educator.

Tanya and Charmaine talk about the journey in support of Maori sovereignty but they admit that sovereignty will not be relinquished by the Crown at the moment. However, they are heartened to hear the government at least acknowledging that Maori have suffered injustices and need restitution.

Charmaine says when money is invested back into Maori hapu, whanau and iwi so that they can claim control of their futures then there will be a chance to talk more about balances of power. She says the word sovereignty is being used in two different ways. "In one sense it means self-determination, personal control over personal destiny, group control over group destiny – the sense of tino rangatiratanga. In the other sense sovereignty means national control or governance.

"Most people can support some form of self-determination if it means less dependency and more competent Maori people doing useful things. People have a lot more struggle about who runs the country. We're going through that struggle with MMP and will do so again over the republican issue.

"Hopefully, in due course we will emerge with quite different forms of control, that are not based on hereditary monarchy or elected presidents, but the concepts of groups of people sharing power and responsibility. A lot of us do it very effectively from day to day at a local level."

Tanya says she does not know how to tackle those issues on a large national scale but she can begin to learn how to work with the local hapu and iwi. "It's an exciting time to be alive in this country and to contribute to shaping the future of New Zealand. What I see happening is a lot of very positive projects and developments involving Maori and Pakeha. There is also a backlash. That is to be expected. But it is nothing to be alarmed about. We just have to keep talking to those people."

Charmaine: "Ngati Te Ata never ceded their sovereignty. Resources and knowledge have been stolen from them but Maori people, as far as I am concerned, still have their sovereignty. The fact is, they are rarely allowed to exercise it. The challenge for Pakeha is to get out of the way and let them get on with exercising it as they did before they were so rudely interrupted."

### GEORGE CHAMBERS

*"THERE ARE TWO HUNDRED PIECES OF LEGISLATION IN NEW ZEALAND THAT ARE DISCRIMINATORY AND THE 1974 TREATY OF WAITANGI ACT AND THE 1984/85 AMENDMENTS ARE THE WORST OF THE LOT. IT IS THE BIGGEST SINGLE BARRIER TO HARMONIOUS RACE RELATIONS IN THIS COUNTRY."*

George Chambers is President of the One New Zealand Foundation, which organised counter-demonstrations against the occupation of Moutoa Gardens.

His organisation uses the slogan "One Law – One People – One New Zealand" and its major platform is to oppose laws which discriminate on the grounds of race. The foundation does not believe that Maori should receive any special consideration as indigenous people and largely believes that Maori land claims are unjustified.

George Chambers was born in England in 1943 and first visited New Zealand in the late sixties. He liked it so much he and his wife and four youngest children migrated here in 1972.

The family lived first in Devonport where George, a rigger by trade, worked at the naval dockyard. A year later the family moved to Kawerau where for 14 years George was a rigging supervisor on the Tasman extension.

He has six children aged from 22 to 30. George is settled in Mount Maunganui and works in public relations, promoting a small rural town nearby.

In May 1995 George Chambers began travelling back and forth to Whanganui to make a stand against Maori sovereignty. The One New Zealand Foundation staged a counter-demonstration for supporters, in the street outside Moutoa Gardens. "We wanted to show that there was another side to New Zealanders, that it wasn't just the people across in Moutoa Gardens. There were people outside who cared about the opposite point of view. And we stood there all day."

On Anzac Day they staged a march which, in George's estimate, attracted a thousand people. Most of the marchers were Pakeha but George was delighted when "a big Maori guy called Joey" joined the front row and captured wide media attention. "I thought that was really good. We don't get a lot of positive press, to be honest."

George also went down to the marae at Moutoa Gardens to talk to Ken Mair, Tame Iti and others. "I'll talk to anybody and quite happily put our point of view and I listen to their point of view."

He claimed, after his discussions, that the local iwi did not support Nick Tangaroa and Ken Mair and their occupation at the gardens. "The majority of Maori in Whanganui didn't want to know. A lot of them were embarrassed. If there were – and there were – wrongs to be righted, then there's ways and means of doing it and that isn't one of them."

The job as president of the One New Zealand Foundation is what George describes as "a public front". He is constantly lobbying government ministers and MPs and collecting information from various organisations from all over the country. Then he accepts invitations to talk to groups about his views.

"I'm more or less a clearing house for information. When I go to a meeting or somewhere like that, I try and give an outline of what's been happening around here and there, and things people have said and a few facts and figures. I answer questions and bring people up to date as I can."

George says his passion is history. He loves to give people "background and truth about historical facts". Ever since he arrived in New Zealand he has been fascinated by its history. He calls it disgusting that the education system teaches New Zealanders so little about their own history. "My wife will tell you that I probably know 10 times more about New Zealand than most New Zealanders. I've got an interest in the place. I've made it my business to find out things."

George Chambers was a foundation member of the One New Zealand Foundation so he has watched its development over the past eight years –

including a lot of negative publicity. "It has a reputation of being redneck and racist. Doug Graham calls us the New Zealand Mafia."

He admits that there have been people with extreme ideas who have joined the organisation and some of them have been very vocal and prominent. "They did a lot of damage to the organisation and when I took over I vowed and declared I was going to change its image."

Whatever George has done to change its image, the foundation seems to be better supported. The membership has grown from 2800, when he became president, to more than 7000. Most of them are older, retired people – "from New Zealand's golden years when the balance of payments was in our favour and the overseas reserves were second to none – who always believed this country had the best race relations in the world."

"You were told that in school apparently. The fact that it was a bloody lie is beside the point. To them their whole world is crumbling before their eyes and they're frightened. They don't know how to handle it."

Some of the members, he says, are Maori although he cannot state the number. "We deliberately don't keep figures like that. We don't ask people what they are. We feel that should be the last question we should ask."

George frequently talks to groups where there are a large number of Maori present and when he is being critical he talks about the lack of education among Maori people. "Usually an older Maori stands up and says, 'You Pakeha stole my language. I was not allowed to speak Maori at school so my language disappeared.' And I always say, 'The person who brought that in was Sir Apirana Ngata who was Minister of Maori Affairs at the time. The reason he did it was that he was the one who brought compulsory schooling for Maori and after two years he realised it wasn't going to work unless they were forced to speak English.'"

Then George talks about what he sees as a failure in Maori parenting which he says is responsible for low educational achievement among Maori. "It's a crying shame because I don't believe the educational system is letting Maori down, I think the parents are letting the kids down.

"Right from the word go, Maori parents were not supportive of an education for their kids. Maybe the parents were ashamed of their own lack of education. I don't know. Maori have always tended to be self-critical and tend to put themselves down unnecessarily."

The solution, as he sees it, is to expand the Parents as First Teachers programme nationwide. He most certainly does not favour the concept of kohanga reo and kura kaupapa Maori. "That is separatism. There is nothing wrong with teaching Maori but why have a separate school for

Maori? I can think of a couple of countries where that's been practised – South Africa is one, the deep south of the United States is another – and wherever it's been practised it is now outlawed. Why should we be walking backwards?"

George claims that children from kohanga and kura are ill-equipped to come back into the Pakeha system and have difficulty with English. To his mind the concept of separate health systems, separate justice systems and separate schools is untenable.

On the law issue: "What we stand for is one law for all people. We don't want the situation where someone can go up in court on a charge and receive a completely different attitude and sentencing from the bench simply because they are Maori."

On the health issue: "I think this whole issue is blown out of all proportion. A Maori appendix is no different to a Pakeha one. When you look at it, the Maori themselves admit there are no full-blooded Maori which means that everybody at the most is fifty per cent. So what have you got – one side of the body that's Maori and one side that's Pakeha? Does the heart beat on the other side?

"How can someone like Ken Mair, who has got one thirty-second Maori in him, say he's a Maori? This is what we're saying. He's a New Zealander. He's a Kiwi with a large European ancestry and a small Maori ancestry."

He feels so strongly about cultural safety programmes for nurse training that he warns his comments are unprintable. "It's not cultural safety, it's not patient sensitivity, it's Maori radicalism! Call it what it is!" In the Waikato nursing curriculum, he says there was a 40-minute lecture on the Sealord deal. "What relevance has that?"

The Sealord deal has relevance for George's opinions about the current Maori leadership. He says the fisheries settlement was supposed to benefit all Maori but it is benefiting only a few people at the top. "There seems to be an impervious layer up there somewhere because it ain't trickling down. It's power and money and it's going to a very small few."

George claims that Maori leadership generally is "poor and pretty self-centred" and he believes tribalism is a negative factor in Maori development. "All the time they cling to tribalism Maori will never have a single voice. And yet you've got this school, your kaumatua and top echelons, who preach tribalism because they know that if Maori stick to their tribal ways that gives them power. They know that if they let the tribal thing go, their power is gone, and that's why they cling to it."

Tino rangatiratanga, in George's understanding, means the right to determine one's own future and to have control of one's own assets. He does not object to that, because he says he asserts the same rights himself. However, he says that some people deliberately confuse tino rangatiratanga with sovereignty. To his mind the two concepts are entirely different.

"The kaumatua does have a lot of control; not as much these days as he used to. But no laws have stopped that. It is only the evolvement of Maori people that has stopped that. Nobody tells them how to run a marae. It's a self-determination thing. Nobody tells me how to run my business. Nobody tells me how to run my house. It may be a different size, but the context is the same."

As for the Treaty of Waitangi and the colonisation of New Zealand, George believes New Zealand was treated very differently from other British colonies. "Britain had always walked in and said, 'Right, this is mine, thank you. I'll have this.'" However, he says the British were not interested in conquering New Zealand.

"We had Australia. New Zealand was there and it was very nice. But no thanks, we didn't want to know. It was the Maori chiefs who made representation that they wanted the Treaty and they wanted the protection of the British Raj – the troops, whatever.

"And this is what amuses me. That document was cobbled together for that time. They didn't have any great pretensions about principles and that sort of thing. It was something that was done at the time. And I'm a great believer that what we should do now is say, 'OK, it was a good beginning and we have had a lot of very positive benefits out of it, but it's had its time.' New Zealand should now have a new constitution. We should look at the Treaty and take the best bits out of it."

George is adamant that Maori knew they were signing away sovereignty in the Treaty. He says many Maori knew English and many of the missionaries – who were well-meaning – knew Maori. "Maori may not be classed as the most brilliant people in the world, but they are very astute business people. So they knew what they were doing. I'm positive."

He says he has read a lot about colonialism and he believes in the majority of cases, where one country was colonised by another, that the colonists have ended up bringing more benefits than losses – there have been more pluses than minuses.

"New Zealand was a special case. We didn't come here as conquerors. We were invited. The Maori people wanted to trade with us. This is how astute they were; within a few short years they had sloops and barques of their own to trade with Australia and other places. So you're not telling me that someone who is supposedly as thick as the proverbial can do that in a few years and be successful at it."

George is not sympathetic to those who say that Pakeha soon robbed Maori of their economic base by taking away their land. "From what I have read, when the missionaries first came here the biggest reason for the tribal fighting amongst Maori was for food. You have only got to look at Ngai Tahu, their slash and burn policy. Their idea of going and collecting the Sunday roast was to set fire to a thousand acres of bush and go in afterwards and see what they could pick up. That's common knowledge, not something I've dragged up."

As for Maori grievances over lost land, George firmly believes that a lot of it is just "hype and put on". "The majority of Maori people I know are not concerned about any loss of land." If there were shonky deals done, he believes they occurred for everyone, Maori and Pakeha.

"Just south of Mangere the same piece of land was sold seven times by someone – I think it was a Nga Puhi, and yet it wasn't Nga Puhi land. But this guy purported to own the land. This was an 1842 Equiticorp thing. This went on."

George says white people perceive Maori as continuously harping back to wrongs that have been righted. He says Tainui and Ngai Tahu had already received settlements in the 1940s through acts of Parliament which at the time were considered a good deal. He says there is no knowing what will happen to the latest Tainui deal in 20 or 30 years.

"This is one of the negatives that Pakeha have against Maori. They don't seem to be able to call it a day. In 1946 Tainui, if I remember rightly, received £100,000 plus £20,000 per year which at that time was an awful lot of money. It was a deal and it was struck and a lot of people now are looking back and saying, 'You had your settlement.'"

The Waitangi Tribunal, and the legislation which set it up, is a subject that George has been hot about since he joined the One New Zealand Foundation. He foresaw far-reaching potential to divide the country and calls it "the biggest single barrier to harmonious race relations."

"The fact that you have got a tribunal who are the sole arbiters and interpreters of the Treaty and Treaty principles means that the Crown has abrogated its responsibility under the Treaty to the tribunal. A non-elected body is deciding what should be decided by the state.

"And you have a tribunal which you can only access if you are a member of a particular race. If someone lays a claim to the land my house sits on – which they have – and it goes before the tribunal, I cannot go to that court and defend my land."

George acknowledges that his land is not under any real threat because the tribunal cannot make any ruling on private land. "But there's a lot of people who are not informed – elderly people – who get very, very frightened when they hear that all this land is under claim, and it's very upsetting for them. I've been to some meetings and seen older people crying because they're so upset. And they see people like Tame Iti on the TV and somebody wielding a club and smashing a car windscreen and things like that. One of the growth industries around most places these days is locksmiths."

The Maori crime rate is a common topic for George when he talks to a meeting. Again he blames poor education. He says the majority of criminals have difficulty with reading and writing. "One of our Rotary members came home and found his house gutted because a couple of the local [Maori] idiots had gone in to rob the place and their idea of covering their tracks was to set fire to it.

"My wife had a very unpleasant experience down on the beach when she took the dog for a walk. There was a Maori guy there with his dog. Further on she looks up and there he is lying naked, just on the edge of the sand dunes, yelling things at her. She will not walk on the beach on her own any more. I rang the police. They came down and the guy was still there. For God's sake! Talk about thick!"

Despite all his comments about Maori issues, George believes he is tolerant of other races. He says one of his sons is married to a Maori and he has a Maori grandchild on the way. Back home in England he remembers his family as being very tolerant also. For instance, he says, the West Indian people who settled in Britain were regarded as part of the landscape. They "fit in" to the English lifestyle.

"Pakistani and Indian people who came from Idi Amin's Uganda – when he turfed all those thousands out – they tended to be a different kettle of fish. They had no intention, and to this day they don't intend, to assimilate. As far as they're concerned they've brought their country with them and they have set it up in England. There's enclaves right throughout Britain where it is predominantly Pakistani or Asian – and it's a shame."

Assimilation is a concept that George would also apply to New Zealand. For instance, he finds the idea that Maori should have special recognition as tangata whenua completely unacceptable. The One New

Zealand Foundation says Maori cannot expect any special favour above anyone else. Everyone should be New Zealanders first and then Maori, English, German, Asian or Pacific Islander, second.

"We're all born the same and we all have exactly the same chance in life. You have to look at the lessons other countries have learnt the hard way as to what happens when you go down the road of separatism. I'm very disgusted with all our political people because they give great credence to this talk of biculturalism. The very definition of the word 'bi', is to divide, to split, to separate. New Zealand is a multicultural society. Every year we are getting twenty-five to thirty thousand new immigrants."

George says he will argue until he is blue in the face that Maori people are not indigenous to New Zealand. He says they came here as migrants a few hundred years before the Pakeha. "Their history tells it. They're proud of the fact that they came in these seven great canoes."

Anyone who is born here is tangata whenua in his estimation. "I mean, I can't say I'm tangata whenua but my grandkids are and so is anyone else born in New Zealand. That is the literal translation. It has nothing to do with ancestry."

While George talks a lot about Pakeha fear aroused by the demands for Maori sovereignty, he says he is not frightened himself. "I don't think we are about to see a Maori takeover of the country. I have no fears about being murdered in my bed. I don't think they are a big enough force. I think if you counted up all the radicals there's no more than 3000 or 4000 of them."

There are a few Maori radicals that he is worried about – those who went to Libya and Cuba in the seventies. "They were trained in subversion, which is all about burrowing yourself into a position of authority and then using it to your own ends. They came back trained but raw. But look at them today. Look at the positions they're holding. They are the ones that are pulling the strings on the likes of Ken Mair. If you are going to have a tribal system, then the kaumatua are going to have to start taking control and flush out the people like that and show them for what they are.

"There is a small group which we know for a fact are actually orchestrating a lot of these protests that spring up all over the country. They don't just happen. You have got professional agitators in there who will spot a situation or, if they can't, will make a situation and really milk it for all it's worth." He is unwilling, for legal reasons, to name the people he is talking about or to explain exactly how they are exerting their influence.

He admits to being a bit puzzled about why Donna Awatere has joined a right-wing political party like ACT because it is not an obvious vehicle for her. "She is a very powerful figure within ACT from what I am told and people listen to her. She has a good opportunity to sway opinion. She was a very, very vocal and up-front radical. I don't know if she has changed. She may have."

George believes there is a link between the training of Maori in Libya, Cuba and the Soviet Union and the change in tactics which he says occurred in 1982. He says one minute there was talk of an armed insurrection and then overnight the Treaty of Waitangi blossomed into a whole new life. "Suddenly you had a document that had been reviled, disregarded, ignored, of no consequence, suddenly gain such importance it was blown out of all proportion.

"Ever since we've seen a build-up of that. This sort of direct confrontation that we've seen in the last eighteen months is a new phase entirely. We believe there is going to be a whole new offensive."

George's solution is for both sides to sit down and talk without any preconceived notions. "We could sit down and say, 'OK, all past baggage is gone out the window, let's start from today. Let's use history as a lesson for the future.' But we've got to go forward. Maori want to go back and you can't do that, it doesn't work."

From another perspective, he says it is just a matter of getting through the next 50 years because after that everyone will have come together. "Give us another 30 or 40 years of intermarriage – another couple of generations – and we're not going to have a race problem. We'll all be part and parcel of each other."

## GRAHAM ROBERTSON

*"WE HAVE TO AVOID ANY SITUATION WHEREBY THE RESOLUTION OF THESE OLD INJUSTICES IS GOING TO CREATE NEW INJUSTICES BY DISPOSSESSING PRESENT-DAY OWNERS, BECAUSE IT IS NOT JUST MAORI WHO BECOME ATTACHED TO THEIR LAND."*

Graham Robertson is a 50-year-old Canterbury farmer of Scottish Presbyterian background and the current President of Federated Farmers of New Zealand.

His grandfather came to Canterbury from Scotland late last century as a farm worker and saved the money to buy land at Methven which Graham still farms. He and his wife, Nicky Jenkins, have expanded the property to 560 hectares in recent years. They grow crops such as wheat, grass and clover seed, peas, lentils and borage with the help of three staff.

Graham says there are few Maori in his district so his contact with Maori has been minimal. He believes that historically the area where they live was inhospitable for Maori to grow food because it is prone to drought, although pre-European Maori probably camped there on the way to other places. Graham's farm relies heavily on irrigation.

Graham Robertson gave little consideration to Maori issues until he became aware of the Treaty settlements and their implications for farmers over the last 10 years. Since then he says it has been part of his *journey of discovery and learning. When he became the National President in 1993 he decided that Treaty issues would be an important part of his role.*

The development of Graham Robertson's understanding of Maori issues is indicative of a change which is taking place in many farmers' thinking throughout New Zealand. While Graham admits that Federated Farmers still has its fair share of rednecks, it is trying to promote discussion and increase the knowledge of its members about the history of colonisation in New Zealand and the need to redress Maori grievances.

The farming community began to take a more active interest in the nineties when it was apparent that claims to the Waitangi Tribunal could have implications for them. Graham says the government has a difficult situation to resolve because much of the land which was taken from its original Maori owners is now in private hands. He says while land was taken illegally, those who own it now bought it through legal processes and have been given clear title.

"We have to avoid any situation whereby the resolution of these old injustices is going to create new injustices by dispossessing present-day owners, because it is not just Maori who become attached to their land. A family who live on a farm, it's their major asset. They derive their living from that land and it is home. They have as much spiritual attachment to the land as the original Maori owners will have."

When farmers are willing sellers and the government wants to buy their land to return to Maori, Graham says there is no problem. He points to two high country stations at Lake Wakatipu which were bought by the government on the open market and placed in a land bank to settle Ngai Tahu claims. Federated Farmers had no objection.

However, in Northland, a recommendation by the Waitangi Tribunal concerning private land has made local farmers angry. "It has created a situation where logical or illogical as it may be, the market has devalued that land, the government refuses to buy it until they have reached agreement with Te Roroa about the settlement. And in the meantime the farmers are left with no possibility of selling the land to anyone else because the land has been blighted by that recommendation."

Graham says four of the five families involved desperately want to get out. They cannot plan their farming operations because they do not know how long they will be there and they cannot borrow money because the banks tell them the commercial value of their farms has devalued by hundreds of thousands of dollars. In addition, he says, it is disruptive to live in the same community with people who feel they have some right to your property.

The claimants and the Pakeha families have made an attempt to get together and see each other's point of view. Graham says they want to avoid the confrontation which occurred over the Titford farm in the same district. "The Titford family just walked away and the farm is just sitting there."

It is a public perception that Alan Titford asked the government to pay more than his farm was worth, but Graham says Federated Farmers has evidence which suggests there was an error in the valuation and he should have been offered more than he was.

Since the Te Roroa case the government has changed the law so that the Waitangi Tribunal cannot make recommendations on private land. However, Graham says a problem could still arise if a claim is made over private land and there is an expectation that the government is going to purchase it.

Where confiscated land is now in developed farmland, Graham says the improved value must be taken into consideration. "One would expect that the return of land, if it is going to resemble the original loss, will be the unimproved component of the present value, not the total land value. So for every three acres confiscated they would on average, say, expect to get one acre back in a fully improved productive state."

Another issue of concern to farmers is Maori reserved lands in Taranaki which had been leased in perpetuity until the government decided to increase the rentals to market rates, accelerate the rent reviews and plan for eventual return of the lands to their owners. Graham says the properties were previously almost as valuable as freehold land because of the perpetual leases. Farmers report losses in equity of between $100,000 and $600,000.

Graham says the Crown must compensate the farmers. He says Maori are not to blame in any way. He says they have been patient, responsible and sympathetic to the plight of the lessees. He also acknowledges the injustice to Maori of the old leases. "The Maori had no right ever to get the lands back, the lessees could go on renting them forever and the rental was fixed over twenty-one-year periods."

He believes most members of the federation would share his view. "There is an innate sense of fairness in most farmers when it comes to these land matters. We have just recently been discussing a Treaty policy and this is a breakthrough for Federated Farmers. Five or ten years ago, the necks would have been fairly red but it was one of the most constructive debates we have had and there was a massive degree of support that the injustices of the past should be resolved.

"Farming families know what it would feel like to have your land pinched by the government. Farmers have a distinctive distaste for the action of governments, governments interfering with their business in any way, governments interfering with their property rights. So they have an instinctive sympathy for Maori who lost their land. It's not a question of 'The government was able to grab this land and we've got it, tough luck for the Maoris!' There is a deep sense of the injustices Maoris have suffered."

He admits that farmers do not always give this impression in the news media. "But just as the inflammatory statements from a Maori activist will hit the headlines, likewise, with a similar degree of bolshiness, from a cockie. Yet there will be a majority of well-meaning people who want to see the thing sorted out in a dignified fashion. But that doesn't make news."

Graham attended a workshop six years ago to learn more about Maori issues and he is enthusiastic about it. "Like so many issues, where you start off just vaguely knowing about them, it's not until you become more immersed in them that you see the full ramifications. It's much easier for us all to remain ignorant and to oppose something from a position of ignorance. The real problem in our society today is to expose people to the real issues rather than the sort of glib approach which the media might take or the foreshortened approach because they don't have the time to really go into them."

Graham has enjoyed reading about the history of the New Zealand wars through the eyes of author James Bellich. "I'd always had a respect for Maori, for their level of ability. All this nonsense you hear that they're an inferior race! And what his book reinforced for me was not only their intelligence, but the way they used inferior resources to beat the tripe out of the bureaucratic British on occasions. I couldn't help feeling pretty pleased about that."

Looking at the new Treaty policy which is being discussed by Federated Farmers, Graham describes it as having two aspects. One is the sense of injustice they understand and want to see put right. The other is more pragmatic.

The federation sees the need for an efficient tribunal process to sort out the grievances because if the process does not have the confidence of Maori then it provides ammunition for the radicals to take the law into their own hands. "We have to have processes whereby reasonable and responsible Maori leaders can demonstrate to their people that the matters are now being resolved.

"The best defence we have as landowners against this sort of activism would be that the majority of Maori feel they are getting a fair hearing and a fair result. We've got a massive vested interest in ensuring that these issues are resolved peacefully."

At the Moutoa Gardens occupation Graham had the impression that moderates were constraining the activists "to stop being so embarrassing." So, he says, the moderates must feel they are getting a fair deal so they do not lose their mana amongst Maoridom. He urges the government to resource the Waitangi Tribunal adequately and to get things done quickly and properly so "it can be fixed once and for all."

Graham admired the leaders who settled the Tainui claim recently because they decided to get on and do a deal, and make the best of the resources that they will receive to get benefits back to their people. However, once again there were some unhappy local farmers.

"The silly old government goes and confiscates land off farmers under the Public Works Act (admittedly at full market value) on the basis that if the government didn't need the land for the purpose for which it was taken, then the farmers would get it back." When the land was included in the Tainui settlement those farmers were upset. Graham says the government will have to work harder at finding voluntary sellers. If the government had sold the farmers back their land (once again at full maket value) then the money could have been used to buy land elsewhere for the Tainui settlement.

The claim that some Pakeha landowners are living off the spoils from the misdeeds of their forebears is not one that Graham accepts. "Once beyond the generation that inflicted the scurrilous behaviour on the Maoris, it's pretty difficult to implicate the present owners. If you start down that track you would have to confiscate assets from every family that had some nefarious activity in their background – if your ancestor was a pirate or a crook or a highway robber. How far back do you go to recover the booty that your granddad or great-granddad filched? That's got to be in the too-hard basket. We can't take responsibility directly for generations before us."

In the past decade many commentators say that Maori have been hit more than any other group by deregulation and other economic restructuring; moves which were supported and encouraged by Federated Farmers. Graham says New Zealand could not have kept going – "Maori, Pakeha or anyone" – if it had carried on the way it was. He says the economy will serve all of the population well, only if it concentrates on creating real productivity, real wealth and real goods and services.

"We were living in fairyland. Farming was crazy. We were producing thirty-nine million lambs because the government said we should produce them, whether there was a market or not, and the ones we couldn't sell they were turning into fertiliser! We had to change all these state-run departments – Railways, Telecom, the Post Office – which were simply creating jobs for people who should be doing something more productive. Most countries in recent years have been privatising, deregulating and introducing competition; so to say it treated Maori unfairly is wrong."

Graham says farmers also took the brunt of the economic restructuring. Some lost their farms and others came very close to doing so. "In no way was it an effect felt solely by Maori. It was felt more by some sectors than others. It certainly was felt by people with poorer skills. The world has been moving to higher technology and more complex skills – all those things which Maori tend not to do so well in – which are required to survive in this age. So the real issue is one of training and education so that Maoris can have a crack at the jobs.

"There is a sense in New Zealand that we want to take care of people who are down and out. But in doing that we don't want to create a situation where they are dependent on state welfare. That devalues humanity – to have them sitting there drawing a pension from the state to do nothing."

Graham does not believe that Maori demands for sovereignty are linked to discontent about issues like socio-economic status. He says the sovereignty debate has more to do with a trend around the world to recognise indigenous people's rights. He says there are some injustices that are not necessarily Treaty matters. "If the Treaty wasn't there I am sure that we, as New Zealanders, would all be concerned about the socio-economic rating of so many Maoris. They are questions of such fundamental justice that we would not ignore them."

It is his opinion that there was no such thing as Maori sovereignty in the Treaty of Waitangi. He says the Maori had no sense of nationhood at that time and the Treaty was signed between the Crown and a large number of individual tribes.

Graham says that any sense of nationhood that Maori may now wish for is the result of their contact with the British. He takes the view that if British values had not been introduced there would have continued to be a large number of iwi operating independently and not being subject to any law common to the whole nation. "Each was subject to the authority of their own tribe and that was where it started and finished.

"It was an agreement between the Crown and what we might regard now as corporate owners of land. And one thing the Treaty certainly legitimises is the traditional form of Maori ownership.

"Whereas, nowadays, if we had a corporate owner of land you would have a legal entity; you would have shares and shareholders and pieces of paper which record that as an entity, what Maori had was communal title. The iwi was the legal unit. Not legal in the sense of European law, but it was recognised as being a bona fide system of ownership of land. In my opinion, what sovereignty is all about is that it conferred on those iwi the recognition that that was, under British law, an entirely lawful and legally recognised system of ownership of their land."

Graham says in its narrowest sense tino rangatiratanga still means that iwi have total control over the resources recognised by the Treaty as being in their ownership. "However, having given Maori legal title to their land, the government then swept in and abused their side of the deal. The real issue of Maori losing their sovereignty was the injustices perpetrated by the early government."

He believes the iwi who signed the Treaty were agreeing to become part of a nation and they understood that they were gaining a system of law and order and protection from the British Crown. "It must have been an awful shock to them when they found that, rather than getting a system of law from the Crown, they had a government that was acting in a totally scurrilous way in too many instances. They must have felt a massive sense of injustice at being double-crossed."

He says Maori chose to sell some of their land. Some land was sold because Maori wanted independent farmers in their communities. "But there was the land they wanted to hang on to and the dastardly government came and took it off them.

"There were instances of Maoris being executed, poisoned and so forth, in an arbitrary fashion. I'm not sure that anybody can remedy that. But where assets were stolen from a legal entity then they have to be returned."

Maori themselves will need to come up with ideas for structures to restore tino rangatiratanga, in his opinion. He would expect Maori to have as much difficulty finding structures as Pakeha. "It is not surprising to me that we have the Maori Congress and the Maori Council and various factions, because we would have even less chance, I think, to get Pakeha to agree on what structures are suitable for representing Pakeha."

Whatever the structures are, he has some ideas of what they should be aiming for. He says they must aim for success by building self-respect – to show that being Maori is not associated with failure. They must have good role models and they need "a fair go at things".

When Maori as tangata whenua and kaitiaki, wishing to assert their tino rangatiratanga, tell Graham that they should have control of the natural resources, such as water, he finds it a very difficult issue.

"What about my people who are farming in Canterbury, whose farms' productivity is totally dependent on water from the rivers? Water has not been turned into a property in this country. Nobody pays for water. If our farmers wish to renew their water rights they go to the regional council. Maori would say, 'Why not give the water to Maori and we will allocate it?' The problem is that you alienate people such as farmers.

"If the water rights are allocated by a regional council we at least are able to vote for regional councillors. There are procedures in place for the development of regional policy statements and plans. There has to be consultation. We all have the right to have our say. To hand those water rights over to the local iwi would alienate those who are presently using it from any say whatsoever in how the resource was being allocated."

Some assets like water and air, he says, are regarded as being for the common good. In his view they should be owned by the community, controlled by the community and allocated by the community.

Even if water were to become a property right, he cannot accept the idea that Maori should have precedence over anyone else to own it. He says the Resource Management Act recognises that Maori were here first and therefore they should be consulted about the resource. However, he says, they are not given the right of veto.

"If there has been a dictatorship by Pakeha in the past, I am not sure we are going to achieve anything by going the other way and saying that Maori should now run New Zealand. Why should Maori people own the water? Water is so fundamental to the lifeblood of a community that it seems an irrational decision to say that one particular group has priority over another group in its allocation. Does that mean that in a thousand years' time that Pakeha will still be excluded from having any sense of ownership or control or feeling for the Whanganui River?"

His viewpoint on water would be the same for other natural resources like oil, geothermal, gold or pounamu. In his opinion these resources belong to everybody and cannot be claimed under the Treaty of Waitangi.

The concept of kaitiakitanga, in which Maori feel a duty as trustees or guardians of the total environment, must also be limited within a consultative and democratic structure, according to Graham, or "it may open up a big can of worms and visit upon future generations".

He would expect Maori values to change from what they were 150 years ago, along with the changes going on in the rest of society. "They have the option of either joining New Zealand as it is now, or isolating themselves in a time warp.

"There will, of course, be many aspects of their culture which they will continue to preserve which are compatible with modern life, but cultural values are not immutable. In my family it was once the case that the head of the household was the male, but it is a part of my culture which I am now having to give up. Any culture which says that these things are beyond any change and beyond any question is in difficulty."

Having said that, Graham envisages increased co-operation between farmers and Maori, over issues like conservation and areas of cultural significance, in the future. He believes farmers, generally, are sensitive to the need to conserve a "nice patch of bush or a sacred site or anything of that sort". They share Maori concerns about the purity of water and the need to prevent effluent from being discharged into waterways.

"In fact, if anything infuriates farmers, it is when they are not given respect for the fact that they have this conservation ethic and the local council slams a preservation order on them, or puts a designation in a district plan which says they are not allowed to cut down bush which they had no intention of cutting down anyway. The bureaucratic council introduces a regulation to do something which the farmers would cheerfully have done voluntarily."

There are examples where farmers have fenced off urupa, allowed access and shown respect for areas which are important to Maori. Graham says there will always be "odd ratbags who are totally obstructive" but the majority of landowners are very sympathetic. Federated Farmers is promoting this kind of understanding and sensitivity through its new Treaty policy.

He says the most productive approach would be for local Maori to talk to farmers about such issues. "Again, done in a friendly spirit of consultation – because landowners can get quite afraid if they feel that there are people wanting their land and maybe don't understand what it is the Maori are after. So I think it's a matter of keep talking and let everybody have their say, and ensuring that, as far as possible, everyone's aspirations can be met with voluntary co-operation."

Graham says part of the importance of the federation's Treaty policy is the signal to members and the public that farmers are serious about the issues and want to join the dialogue. "We are too easily characterised as rednecks and selfish landowners, when in fact the people I know in farming are very much the opposite. They enjoy their land and they enjoy sharing it, or the use of it, as far as possible, with other people."

When the Treaty policy was debated among 150 farmer delegates at their 1995 conference, Graham says there was great unanimity and a tremendous atmosphere.

"The ones who go to Wellington may not be representative of everyone back home, I would accept that, but certainly the sense of spirituality, the sense of really getting to the deep issues, came through very strongly and it was a powerful experience for me to chair that.

"It is one of the things we have to get right. After all, Federated Farmers represents the largest group of private landowners in the country, so we have got a big stake in getting the injustices sorted out in a dignified and proper way."

### ROGER TAFA

*"I SUPPORT MAORI SOVEREIGNTY. BUT IT IS UP TO MAORI TO DECIDE FOR THEMSELVES WHAT THEY MEAN BY SOVEREIGNTY. EVEN IF THAT MEANS SETTING UP A SEPARATE STATE, THAT'S SOMETHING I BELIEVE PEOPLE SHOULD SUPPORT."*

**R**oger Tafa is a young Auckland University graduate who has actively supported Maori sovereignty by protesting at Pakaitore and Tamaki College.

He was born in Whangarei in 1967 and lived there until he moved to Auckland to study. He is now employed in the university's audio visual unit.

Roger's father was part of the first big wave of Western Samoan immigrants who came to Auckland in the early 1950s. His mother is a teacher of Scottish/Nova Scotia heritage. Roger's father mixed with the few other Samoans in Whangarei and had many Maori mates at the Marsden Point oil refinery and glass factory where he worked. Roger and his mother also made many Maori friends.

Being brown meant that Roger was always mistaken for a Maori so he came to identify with the tangata whenua rather than to think of himself as Pakeha or Tauiwi. "As the years go by I would hope that New Zealanders with a Pacific Island background will identify more and more with the tangata whenua."

One of Roger Tafa's first involvements with Maori activism was the protest at Waitangi during the 1990 commemorations. He was 22. "We all massed at Paihia Wharf and marched around to Waitangi and were confronted with several rows of police with batons. They were determined that no one was going to get across and there was pushing and shoving and batons drawn and several arrests."

The non-Maori in the protest were from groups like Project Waitangi and AFIA. Roger was there with comrades from Workers' Power. "The Maori welcomed our supporting role and were thankful that we identified with the struggle."

Well before that day Roger had made a commitment to work against racism. He says he understood what racism felt like. As a teenager in Whangarei he had found himself frequently identified by the police as Maori.

"You had to face the continual police harassment. Walking anywhere at night or even sitting down talking to people – 'loitering' – meant that you were an immediate target for police harassment. It was common for me and my friends to be pulled over in cars, searched without warrants, strip searched. I had friends who were physically attacked by the police. It was accepted knowledge that this is what you could expect from the police in Whangarei at the time."

It made Roger angry and spurred him into "analysing society" and into taking political action. It was one major reason why he became a socialist, coupled with another important influence in his young life – the Springbok tour of 1981.

"I was only thirteen but I remember all the events around it. I remember my mother and her friends being involved in the protest and it was also a time when I read Steve Biko's biography by Donald Woods, which played quite a prominent role in my memory."

The Springboks played against North Auckland in Whangarei and the divisions their tour created in Roger's own community showed him that racism was not confined to South Africa. He has a vivid picture of his mother standing behind the big rows of barbed wire and police as a protester, while some of her teacher colleagues on the other side of the barricade were going into the football game.

"When you see teachers who in a normal situation get on fine but where some were going in and other teachers were yelling 'Shame!' and all sorts of other things at them, it makes you realise that we do live in a society that is divided by race and where racism exists."

Later, Roger was also influenced by the American black power movement. At university he found that there was some common identity among young educated Pacific Islanders and Maori based on black consciousness. "The revival of those ideas that have re-emerged around Malcolm X and the Black Panthers has led to a much higher awareness in New Zealand among Samoan and Pacific Island people. They can recognise that that's also a feature of their lives."

Black consciousness is backed by a popular youth culture as well as its political aspects. It has its own methods of communication, the casual way of talking interspersed with words like "bro", "hey wassup?" and "the man", the high fives and the hand slaps. Maori and Pacific Island youth also identify with the black music that goes with the culture – soul, jazz, hip hop and reggae.

Roger acknowledges that the Samoan community as a whole does not align itself with Maori aspirations. "Samoan families and communities can be very insular, based on the traditional tribal/clan type of relationship, so anyone from outside of that is outside. There are derogatory views even about other Pacific Island groups such as Tongans. I'm sure that is the case for Maori also.

"There is in the Samoan community the idea that is associated particularly with urban Maori – you know, the gang thing and the propaganda you get about Maori being criminals, gang members and unemployed etcetera. Because Samoan families are very community-based they see the urban Maori as having rejected that sort of tribal and family based life. The Samoan community is just as influenced by the media as any other non-Maori group."

Roger is glad he had the experience of growing up in Whangarei, although he has some regrets about gaps in his knowledge about his own Samoan background. As a boy he visited Western Samoa twice and he understands some conversational Samoan but cannot speak, read or write it. He would like to know more but he says he is not in an environment where he can practise and learn.

"It helps me to empathise with the loss of language and culture in Maoridom. The attempt by Maori so far to protect their language, customs and cultural heritage is a very positive thing and something that everyone should support.

"The Samoan identity and culture is secure in Samoa, their homeland. But for Maori in New Zealand there is nowhere else they can go to assert that identity. Even in New Zealand, in a city like Auckland, the Samoan structures are really tight, whereas for a lot of urban Maori there is no longer any association with their rural or tribal heritage."

Roger says cultural loss and the Maori position in society "as an oppressed minority" are reasons for the low educational achievement of Maori. "Schools are only factories for turning out the ideas and sort of people that society wants and needs and if you are a Maori or Pacific Islander you are going to be a worker or unemployed. It's a legacy of colonialism which has pushed them into a corner which is not of their own making."

Many Samoan families place great importance on educating their children. It is often one of the reasons they migrated to New Zealand. Roger's father is typical. He had little formal education himself so he raised Roger with the idea that if you have education behind you, you can do whatever you like.

"Some people have the simplistic idea that Maori don't have high educational achievement based on ignorance, lack of motivation or apathy. That doesn't take into account economic and social factors. It is a very different perspective for people who have come to New Zealand specifically to get their children an education."

Roger did not share his father's enthusiasm for education when he first went to Auckland University in 1985. He was there largely because his friends were studying too. "To my surprise I managed to pass four papers, so I decided to go back the next year. The following year I passed four papers again. So I thought, well, I've got eight papers I might as well finish my degree." He majored in sociology.

Although he had been surrounded by Maori neighbours, friends and schoolmates in Whangarei, Roger cannot remember any formal education about Maori history during his years at school there. It was not until he took sociology, education and history papers at university that he learnt anything about the past and how it had affected Maori.

"It gives you a much firmer basis of understanding. The more you look at history, you become confirmed in your views. For me, learning about it was confirmation that here is a just struggle, something I could support. Anyone who calls themselves a consistent democrat could not help but see the injustice and would want to see it corrected. They could not help but support self-determination."

Roger agrees with the concept of Maori sovereignty because he says everyone in New Zealand has a duty to address some of the grievances and injustices that have occurred historically and continue today. "But it is up to Maori to decide for themselves what they mean by sovereignty. Even if that means setting up a separate state that's something I believe people should support."

Sovereignty for him does not mean the Sealord deal or the Tainui settlement. They are not a serious attempt to redress the past as far as he is concerned. "What is handed over so far you couldn't say constituted any economic base that Maori as a whole could subsist or survive on. It's very much the Maori leaderships, negotiators and leaders of trust boards that are the ones who will benefit from those deals; the Mahutas and the O'Regans. It's not going to affect urban Maori or rural Maori much. It is going to heighten the class divisions within Maoridom as well."

Roger points to some complex issues to be resolved. He says the division of the fishing quota is an example. Should it be divided up on a coastal model or population model or what? He claims that it is part of the government strategy to create conflicts, to make Maori vie for bits and pieces. It takes the heat off themselves. Also to be faced, in his opinion, is the urban versus rural issue and the accountability of the iwi and trust boards. "Most of them aren't democratic in the formal sense. A lot are appointments and not by election. There's conflict between the rank and file and the leaderships."

For this reason Roger would find it hard to accept Maori sovereignty in the form of hereditary chiefs. "My father would probably have more respect for hereditary chiefs but I'm a socialist. People have a right to practise their culture, if that means the chiefly system, whether it be matai or rangatira, that's up to them. But I don't think someone should be a leader just because they are the chief or the chief's son, or appointed by the chief. I think leaders should be elected by the people they're claiming to represent and they should be accountable and recallable."

Early in 1995 Roger helped form a new group called the Aotearoa Action Coalition which was a united front of non-Maori who wanted to play a part in the opposition to the fiscal envelope proposals.

"I became involved personally because I have been actively involved in socialist politics and this was an issue that I was concerned about and looking to get active around. The coalition was a vehicle. A lot of non-Maori were pissed off about the fiscal envelope as well, but didn't know what they could do or how they could support the struggle."

As a Samoan, Roger can see many avenues for Maori and Pacific Islanders to unite on issues that affect them commonly; for instance, the dispute over the old Tamaki Girls' College in Auckland. He says it was clearly a multi-ethnic community resource that was being used particularly by Maori and Pacific Islanders. When the school was about to be sold by the Ministry of Education the two groups united in protest.

"I think that shows that there is a basis for unity. Being where they are on the socio-economic ladder will always mean there will be chances for that common cause to come up. I went out there to support the protest through the Aotearoa Action Coalition."

Roger went to Whanganui to support the Pakaitore occupation, too. He and two other Pakeha members of the coalition went with a contingent organised by Te Kawau Maro. They responded to the call for support when the city council's eviction deadline came up at the end of March. He found the experience positive because of the display of unity and common cause and believes it may lead to other occupations in the future.

His only disappointment was the absence of any real union support. This he puts down to the state of the unions and their leadership since the Employment Contracts Act. "They've been hesitant and reticent to stick their necks out on any issue let alone the issues facing their own members. I thought there might have been more union involvement given that Niko Tangaroa [one of the Pakaitore leaders] was a prominent unionist."

Roger's assessment of the Treaty of Waitangi may be at odds with some of the Maori activists. The old slogan "The Treaty of Waitangi is a fraud!" is the correct one according to him. He says the government cannot honour the Treaty as it exists. "It was only ever a device to defraud and deny Maori. It's been one of the main vehicles for colonisation of this country."

In his view the 1835 Declaration of Independence states the issues more clearly but is conveniently ignored in favour of the Treaty. He believes the government has no intention of honouring it in any serious way, yet the Treaty is being used as a diversion to buy off some of the leadership.

"When the Labour government first brought in the Waitangi Tribunal legislation it took the protest off the streets and it became a paper chase through the courts, submissions and inquiries and research and whatever. I think it was a step back for the movement and it forced them to confront the state on its own terms, through its own courts, through its own legal processes."

He still supports all the claims and struggles that have been articulated in terms of the Treaty. However, to hold up the Treaty itself as the document that will solve all problems is pointless in his mind. He says

Maori need to be able to build something that has been denied them for so long – an economic base and political power and control over it.

In his university environment Roger finds little real evidence of progress in dealing with Maori sovereignty. He says despite its "liberal pretence" the university is not setting any examples of power sharing. He can support the efforts the university has made in the area of positive discrimination but believes that until the root causes are dealt with it comes across as tokenism.

He dismisses the idea that such institutions can devolve enough power to Maori within the existing structures to make it significant. "Ultimately, it's just a reformist dream that you can change a state structure as they exist simply by replacing a few white faces with a few brown faces. Ultimately the state and those structures exist for a purpose and for the defence of a certain social order. Until you challenge the basis of the whole state then those reforms are going to be only token.

"It takes socialism which means revolution, in the sense that power is transferred from those who wield it and from the state that they control, and given to the majority of the population that create the wealth. Revolutions historically exist once a social crisis gets to a point where it has to be decided one way or the other – revolution or counter-revolution."

New Zealand's social crisis is not acute enough yet for his scenario to take place. However, he predicts a time when people will seek out more radical solutions than are presently available or even thought about. "While revolution and socialism are not the agenda for tomorrow, I think it's the only goal that ultimately will solve the problem for Maori and the working class as a whole."

It may mean violence, he says. Violence is something that conjures up different images for different people. He sees the violence of the state. "We live in a society which promotes daily violence. Chronic long-term unemployment, poverty, restructuring in health and education, the move to market rents in state housing – to me these are all acts of violence, of persecution. It's the acts of one class against another. So it's usually a case of self-defence."

Roger's strong opinions are delivered in a softly spoken, understated manner but he offers Maori struggling for sovereignty an active solidarity based on his socialist principles. "Until there is a totally free and co-operative and socialised society, only then will Maori grievances be addressed."

# GLOSSARY

| | |
|---|---|
| ariki | paramount chief |
| aroha | love |
| e noho | sit down |
| hapu | sub-tribe |
| hei konei ra | goodbye |
| hui | meeting or gathering |
| kaitiaki; kaitiakitanga | trustee or guardian; the duty of trusteeship for present and future generations |
| kanuka | giant tea tree |
| kaumatua | elder |
| kawa | protocol |
| kawana; kawanatanga | Governor (transliteration); function of government, governance, government |
| kereru | wood pigeon |
| kohanga reo | Maori language early childhood institute, language nest |
| kuia | old lady |
| kura | school |
| mana | authority, prestige, power |
| mana motuhake | separate and independent authority |
| mana whenua | authority over land |
| manuhiri | visitor(s) |
| marae | traditional village |
| matua | father, parent |
| mokopuna | grandchild, grandchildren |
| pa | fortified place or settlement |
| pakeha | a person of predominantly British or, more latterly, European descent |

| | |
|---|---|
| pounamu | greenstone |
| putea | fund |
| rangatira | chief |
| rangatiratanga | chieftainship, authority (often translated as sovereignty, self determination, autonomy etc) |
| raupatu | confiscation |
| rohe | tribal area or boundary |
| rohe pooti | Maori regional council proposed by the Alliance party |
| runanga | assembly or council |
| taha | side or part |
| taihoa | by and by |
| tangata whenua | people of the land |
| tangihanga | funeral |
| taonga | treasure(s) |
| tauiwi | foreigner |
| tikanga | custom, rule or values |
| tino rangatiratanga | absolute authority or chieftainship (otherwise translated as independence, sovereignty, self-determination etc) |
| tino | very |
| tohunga | expert, priest |
| tokotoko | staff or walking stick |
| tupuna | ancestor |
| turangawaewae | place to stand |
| urupa | burial ground |
| whakapapa | genealogy |
| whanau | family, extended family |

# About the author

Carol Archie worked for 25 years as a journalist in television news, current affairs and documentaries. Now a freelance journalist, she moves between TV, radio and print as a writer, director, narrator and interviewer. She has been involved in documentaries on diverse subjects such as pesticides, the Cartwright enquiry, Asian immigration and women's issues. In 1994, she directed the television documentary on family violence *Not Just a Domestic*.

Carol's interest in Maori life and politics began in the late seventies. She has reported on many Maori issues for television news and current affairs. In 1988 she travelled to Canada and the USA to make television programmes comparing the sovereignty and land rights issues of native Americans with those of Maori. Her freelance work includes reporting for Mana Maori Media on a regular basis. Recently she made radio documentaries for iwi stations after attending hui throughout New Zealand as tribes were consulted about the allocation of fishing assets and the government's fiscal envelope proposals.

Carol's forebears came to New Zealand four and five generations ago. *Maori Sovereignty - The Pakeha Perspective* is her first book. She and her husband live in the country near Auckland.

Front and back cover photographs by John McDermott.